LEWIS and CLARK

Songs of the Journey
Companion

LEWIS and CLARK
Songs of the Journey Companion

Kindra Ankney

Edge-of-the-Woods Publishing
Yakima, Washington

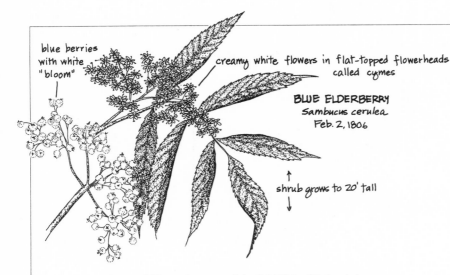

blue berries with white "bloom"

creamy white flowers in flat-topped flowerheads called cymes

BLUE ELDERBERRY
Sambucus cerulea
Feb. 2, 1806

↑ shrub grows to 20' tall ↓

Pressed plants on cover:
(front) vine maple, camas
(back) western redcedar, bitterroot

Edge-of-the-Woods Publishing
PO Box 8251
Yakima, Washington 98908

Quotations taken from:

Original Journals of the Lewis and Clark Expedition, Volumes 1-7, edited by Reuben Gold Thwaites.
Dodd, Mead & Company, 1904-1905; reprinted in 2001 by Digital Scanning, Inc., Scituate, MA.

The Journals of the Lewis & Clark Expedition, Volumes 2, 9, and 10, edited by Gary Moulton.
University of Nebraska Press, 1986-1996. (Lewis (1803), Ordway, and Gass)

Letters of the Lewis and Clark Expedition, with Related Documents: 1783-1854, edited by Donald Jackson.
University of Illinois Press, 1962. (Jefferson, August 18, 1813)

Publishers Cataloging in Publication
Ankney, Kindra
    Lewis and Clark: songs of the journey companion / Kindra Ankney.—1st ed.
    p. 128   cm. 23
    Includes bibliographical references and index.
1. Lewis and Clark Expedition (1804-1806). 2. Lewis, Meriwether, 1774-1809.
3. Clark, William, 1770-1838. 4. West (U.S.)—Discovery and exploration. I. Title.

F592.7.A55 2003
917.804'2—dc21

ISBN 0-9708434-1-0 (paperback)
Library of Congress Control Number: 2002096065

Printed in the United States of America

To my husband and children

Acknowledgements

Acknowledgements are first due to the following interpretive centers and museums for providing a wealth of information: Fort Clatsop National Memorial, Astoria, OR; Columbia River Maritime Museum, Astoria, OR; Lewis and Clark Interpretive Center at Fort Canby State Park, Ilwaco, WA; Fort Vancouver National Historic Site, Vancouver, WA; The Columbia Gorge Interpretive Center Museum, Stevenson, WA; Columbia Gorge Discovery Center, The Dalles, OR; Chelan County Historical Society Museum, Cashmere, WA; Yakama Nation Museum, Toppenish, WA; Nez Perce National Historical Park, Spalding, ID; Lewis and Clark National Historic Trail Interpretive Center, Great Falls, MT; Knife River Indian Villages National Historic Site, Stanton, ND; The North Dakota Lewis & Clark Interpretive Center, Washburn, ND; Illinois State Museum, Springfield, IL; National Museum of American History, Smithsonian Institution, Washington, DC; Missouri Historical Society, St. Louis, MO; American Museum of Natural History (AMNH), New York, NY; The Maritime Museum, Newport News, VA; Peabody Museum of Archaeology and Ethnology, Harvard University, Cambridge, MA.

To the many kind folks who willingly shared their time, knowledge, and sometimes even personal resources in assisting with research, a sincere thank you: Nancy Eid, Jill Harding, Janice Elvidge, William Maxwell, Robert Moore, Diane Mallickan, Linda Paisano, Jeffrey Smith, Patrice Tunge, Kevin Kirky, Mike Scholl, Gary Lentz, Amy Mossett, Mary Dodds Schlick, Huel Willis, Jeremy Skinner, Johnny Clark, and James Day.

For thoughtfully reading the manuscript and making many helpful suggestions and corrections, my heartfelt gratitude to Jeanene Hunt, Sally Freeman, Dr. Larry McClure, Kara Clark, Beth and Warren Sharp, Daniel Slosberg, Dorothy Cook, Kevin Peters, Drucilla Gould, Janiece Bates, Cultural Resource Specialist Barbara Minard, and C. Lawrence Cooper, Ph.D.

Thanks also to my parents and parents-in-law for loving encouragement and to dear friends for offering words of cheer at just the right time: Elaine Brennecke, Sheri Gordon, Elizabeth Stump, Dee Fleming, Sharon Glenn, Kelly Casebeer, and Dorry Eldon. A word of appreciation also to Claudia Nice who, through her books, taught me to love pen and ink.

A humongous thank you to Bobby Horton: Working with you has been a pleasure; getting to know you, a delight.

And to my sweet family—Sam, Jamin, and Emily: Thank you so much for hours and hours of sacrifice, for helping out when time was short, for listening to endless brainstorming sessions, for adventurously trying out recipes and tirelessly traveling the trail, for your unwavering support and faithful prayers, for being channels of His blessing. Without you this book would never have been completed.

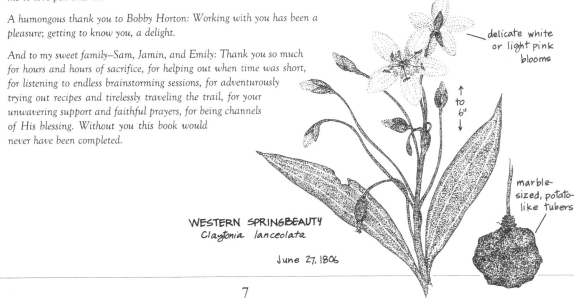

delicate white or light pink blooms

to 6"

WESTERN SPRINGBEAUTY
Claytonia lanceolata

June 27, 1806

marble-sized, potato-like tubers

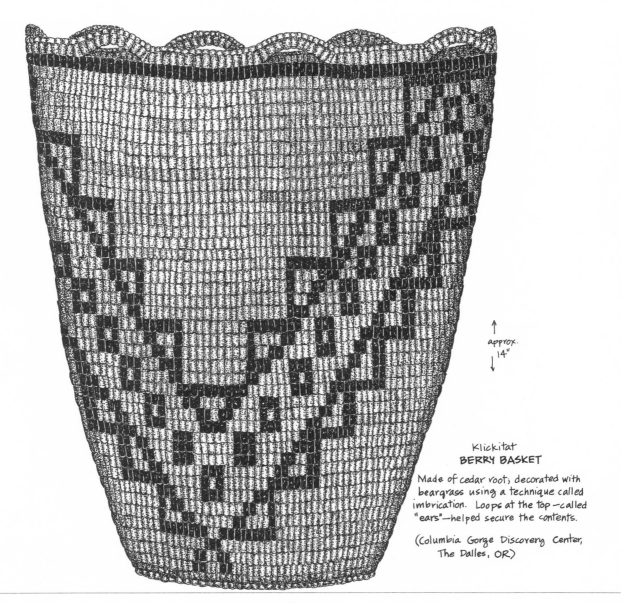

↑
approx.
14"
↓

Klickitat
BERRY BASKET

Made of cedar root; decorated with
beargrass using a technique called
imbrication. Loops at the top —called
"ears"—helped secure the contents.

(Columbia Gorge Discovery Center,
The Dalles, OR)

Contents

PACIFIC BLACKBERRY
Rubus ursinus

Mar. 25, 1806

Glossy, black fruit;
each berry consists of many
small drupes or "drupelets."

—drupelets

notched,
pink petals

SHOWY PHLOX
Phlox speciosa

May 7, 1806

Activities

Working with the same types of materials and objects used during the expedition is a rewarding experience. The feel of soft buckskin, the jangle of a deer-toe rattle, or the simple beauty of a pressed flower help us appreciate more fully the sights and sounds encountered on the trail. There are many such creative opportunities in a study of the Lewis and Clark Expedition. The activities in this book are just a beginning. **Some are appropriate for all ages, others require adult supervision.** See page 120 for suppliers of materials.

Recipes

Because the captains regularly mentioned daily meals, we have an ongoing record of what the Corps of Discovery ate and even an occasional description of how foods were prepared. Kettles of various sizes were taken for boiled dishes; some meals were roasted, some were fried, and still others were pulled from knapsacks or "possibles" pouches to be eaten cold. Changes in geography dictated diet variations. Game meats (particularly buffalo, elk, and deer) were consumed through the Upper Plains, but became scarce through the Rocky Mountains. Fish—especially in its dried form—was available west of the Rockies and on to the Pacific Ocean, where elk once again became regular fare. Cultivated vegetables were purchased from the Upper Missouri River tribes, wild roots and berries from the people of the Plateau and Northwest Coast region. Each area, through its abundance or the generosity of its people, brought continued nourishment to the corps.

Designed to give a culinary glimpse into the simple foods of the expedition, the recipes in this book use (for the most part) ingredients similar to those that were purchased prior to the expedition or that became available along the way. Most of the ingredients can be purchased at grocery or health food stores; page 120 lists sources for harder-to-find items. **Young cooks must have adult supervision.**

4 - 4½"

BROAD-TAILED HUMMINGBIRD
Selasphorus platycercus

June 15, 1806

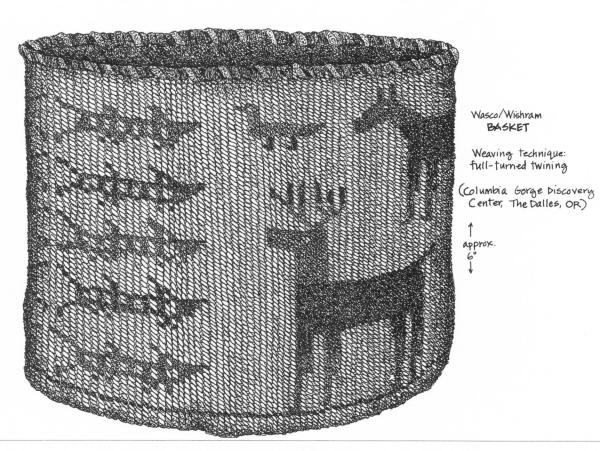

Wasco/Wishram
BASKET

Weaving technique:
full-turned twining

(Columbia Gorge Discovery
Center, The Dalles, OR)

↑
approx.
6"
↓

12

Introduction

Little did I know back in 1997 that the Lewis and Clark Expedition study my children had embarked upon would become a consuming, long-term fascination for the entire family. We read books and watched documentaries, read more books and visited interpretive centers. Soon we found ourselves searching for expedition plants and animals, then building our own journals based on their scientific discoveries. By this time we were thoroughly captivated with the tale. We made tallow candles and buffalo jerky and flour from Oregon white oak acorns; we parched corn, learned to play the jew's harp, and *tried* to start a fire with flint and steel. What began one day as a simple writing assignment expanded to become a song. An entire series of songs soon followed, then a musical CD, and now, at last, a book to pull it all together.

One of the most beautiful things we found about the story of the expedition is that it holds something of interest for nearly everyone: flora, fauna, and Native American cultures; period weaponry, music, and cooking methods; mapmaking, hide tanning, and canoe building; geography, geology, archeology ... The list goes on and on, each area full of potential for personal discovery. This book is a sampler of topics that my family and I found particularly interesting as we explored through the lens of Lewis and Clark.

Creating the pen-and-ink illustrations found within these pages was a delight. By drawing in detail, just as the captains did in their journals, I gained new admiration for their first-hand experiences and keen observation skills. Many of the drawings are based on photos taken during family outings; others were sketched in the field and finished at home. Several of the botanical and zoological illustrations have dates written by them; these dates, based on Paul Russell Cutright's book *Lewis & Clark: Pioneering Naturalists*, indicate Lewis and Clark's first recorded encounter with (or description of) that particular plant or animal.

This volume is intended as a complement to Bobby Horton's musical recording of *Lewis and Clark: Songs of the Journey*. The chapters correspond to each of the fifteen songs on the recording, picking up where the lyrics leave off to complete the story. Along with the text are quotes upon which the songs are based, taken directly from expedition journals and other historical documents. (Because American English spelling had not been completely standardized in the early 1800s, the reader will notice many irregular—and sometimes colorful—spellings within the quotations.) Also included in the book are activities and recipes to enhance the study of Lewis and Clark, along with related sidebars.

Our lives have been made richer, and our appreciation for America's heritage made deeper, through learning about the Corps of Discovery. It is my sincere hope that others will enjoy a similar adventure with *Lewis and Clark: Songs of the Journey* and this companion volume.

Kindra Ankney

6-14"

May 8, 1806

YELLOW FAWN LILY
Erythronium grandiflorum

"Honored Parents:
I now embrace this oportunity of writing to you once more to let you
know where I am and where I am going. I am well thank God and in high Spirits.
I am now on an expedition to the westward, with Capt Lewis and Capt Clark,
who are appointed by the President of the united States to go on an Expedition
through the interior parts of North America,   we are to ascend the Missouri River
with a boat as far as it is navigable and then go by land to
the western ocean, if nothing prevents."
JOHN ORDWAY, April 8, 1804

THE CORPS OF DISCOVERY

When Thomas Jefferson proposed an expedition to explore the western half of the North American continent, he envisioned a group of ten to twelve members headed by a strong, intelligent leader. As plans unfolded, however, the size of group needed for such an undertaking grew considerably. The leadership also grew: Rather than having one captain, there would be two—an unusual military arrangement.

One of President Jefferson's main goals for this venture was to find, if possible, a continuous navigable river route that could be used for transportation and trade from one side of the continent to the other. He hoped to forge ties with the native people who inhabited the land and who could furnish "great supplies of furs and peltry." He saw it as a voyage of discovery that would advance science and increase geographic knowledge.

This wouldn't be the first attempt to ascend the Missouri and cross the continent. Previous explorers—from other countries as well as the United States—had tried. But this time would be different. The President was determined that it would succeed. On January 18, 1803, he sent a secret message to Congress requesting authority to pursue the endeavor.

"The object of your mission is to explore the Missouri river, & such principal stream of it, as, by it's course & communication with the waters of the Pacific Ocean, may offer the most direct & practicable water communication across this continent, for the purposes of commerce."

THOMAS JEFFERSON
June 20, 1803

BEAVER
Castor canadensis

The Corps of Discovery

Captains Lewis and Clark
Explored this great land,
Thirty-three people
An adventurous band.
They went to discover a passage to the sea,
Our great growing country
Depended on that key.

They started this adventure in 1804;
Two years, four months, ten days,
Eight thousand miles went the corps.
Three hundred new plants and animals
Recorded by their hand;
Many different Indian tribes
Met this peaceful band.

Oh, the Corps of Discovery
Mapped the great Northwest;
Oh, the Corps of Discovery—
A triumphant success!

*"I am instructed to select
from any corps in the army a
number of noncommissioned
officers and privates not
exceeding 12, who may be
disposed voluntarily to enter into
this service; and am also
authorized to engage any other
men not soldiers that I may
think usefull in promoting the
objects or success of this
expedition...it shall be my duty
by enquiry to find out and
engage some good hunters,
stout, healthy, unmarried men,
accustomed to the woods,
and capable of bearing
bodily fatigue in a pretty
considerable degree"*

MERIWETHER LEWIS
June 19, 1803

*"from the nature of this
enterprise much must depend
on a judicious scelection
of our men"*

MERIWETHER LEWIS
August 3, 1803

Into this Service
"thirty-three people, an adventurous band..."

Members of the Corps of Discovery included rugged outdoorsmen skilled in boating, hunting, trapping, and interpreting. Some were carpenters. Others were black-smiths. All were courageous and "capable of bearing bodily fatigue." Two of them were brothers, two were cousins, and three had wives at home. Their ages spanned two-and-a-half decades: The youngest enlisted man, George Shannon, was in his late teens; the oldest, John Shields, was thirty-five. Most were twenty-five to thirty-five years old. The party included an African-American—Captain Clark's slave, York—and men of Irish, French, French-Canadian, German, Native American, Scottish, and Welsh descent.

When the expedition set out from their 1803-1804 winter camp near St. Louis, more than forty adventurers were on board. Most were soldiers, some newly enlisted, who would remain with the corps throughout the entire journey. Several were rivermen of French descent, called *engagés* or *voyageurs*, who had been hired to help transport the boats up the Missouri. After the following winter at Fort Mandan, twenty-nine of the original members continued on in what is now referred to as the "permanent party." With the addition of the Charbonneau family (Toussaint Charbonneau, Sacagawea, and their baby, Jean Baptiste) and Jean Baptiste LePage, all of whom joined at Fort Mandan, the permanent party totaled thirty-three. Those who didn't go on with the Corps of Discovery returned to St. Louis.

"all well, raised a Flag"
WILLIAM CLARK
September 25, 1804

Fifteen-Star Flag of the United States

Although there were seventeen states in 1804, the flag that was hoisted over expedition camps had only fifteen stars. (In 1818, Congress adopted the current design that represents each state of the Union with a star.) The fifteen-star, fifteen-stripe flag is *the* Star-Spangled Banner that inspired Francis Scott Key to pen what would one day become our national anthem.

PERMANENT PARTY ROSTER

Captain William Clark   Captain Meriwether Lewis

FIRST SQUAD	SECOND SQUAD	THIRD SQUAD
Sergeant Nathaniel Pryor	Sergeant Patrick Gass*	Sergeant John Ordway
Pvt. George Gibson	Pvt. Hugh McNeal	Pvt. William Bratton
Pvt. George Shannon	Pvt. Joseph Field	Pvt. John Colter
Pvt. John Shields	Pvt. Reubin Field	Pvt. Alexander Willard
Pvt. John Collins	Pvt. John B. Thompson	Pvt. William Werner
Pvt. Joseph Whitehouse	Pvt. Richard Windsor	Pvt. Silas Goodrich
Pvt. Peter Weiser	Pvt. Robert Frazer	Pvt. John Potts
Pvt. Pierre Cruzatte	Pvt. Jean Baptiste LePage	Pvt. Hugh Hall
Pvt. Francois Labiche		
Pvt. Thomas P. Howard		

NON-MILITARY MEMBERS

George Drouillard, York, Toussaint Charbonneau, Sacagawea, Jean Baptiste Charbonneau

*Patrick Gass was promoted to sergeant on August 26, 1804, after the death of Sergeant Charles Floyd.

Each member of the expedition played a part in its success, but there were several whose contributions were especially noteworthy. Patrick Gass was an experienced carpenter whose building skills were of much benefit on the journey, especially when constructing winter quarters. John Shields was a gunsmith and a carpenter, but his service as a blacksmith was particularly valuable. During the winter at Fort Mandan, his iron creations were traded for a steady supply of food. George Drouillard, son of a French-Canadian father and a Shawnee mother, furnished sign language interpretation with Native Americans. It was his expert hunting skills, however, that made him an indispensable member of the expedition. Other exceptional hunters included brothers Joseph and Reubin Field, John Colter, and John Collins. Additional interpretation was provided by Sacagawea, Toussaint Charbonneau, Francois Labiche, and Pierre Cruzatte. Cruzatte was also the chief boatman and fiddle player. John Ordway contributed to the success of the corps in a variety of ways. His duties included issuing provisions, keeping records, and, in the absence of the captains, taking command.

CORPS OF
DISCOVERY
is a shortened version of
"CORPS OF VOLUNTEERS
FOR NORTH WESTERN
DISCOVERY"

ORDERLY BOOK
August 26, 1804

May 14, 1804 - September 23, 1806
"two years, four months, ten days..."

The expedition officially started in May of 1804, but preparations had begun in earnest much earlier—once congressional authority was given. Objectives were defined, expert advice was sought. So that no detail would be forgotten, lists were created: of anticipated needs, of expenses, of inquiries concerning the "Indians of Louisiana."

Building a strong team took time and careful attention. Many wanted to join; only those who passed an exacting inspection were selected. At winter camp on Wood River (known as Camp Wood or Camp Dubois), the men were assigned hard work and given opportunities to sharpen their shooting skills. Rigid military discipline prepared them for the "vast enterprise" ahead.

Sixteen months of purposeful readying preceded the 28-month, 8,000-mile journey.

HUNTING POUCH
Carries lead balls, extra flints, tinder box, etc.

Firearms Used on the Expedition

"The practicing party will...discharge only one round each p'. day...all at the same target...of fifty yards"
DETACHMENT ORDERS, Camp River Dubois, February 20, 1804

AIRGUN
Because it operated using compressed air rather than spark and powder, the airgun was an astonishing novelty. Captain Lewis fired it to impress the native people.

FIFTEEN RIFLES from the
HARPERS FERRY ARSENAL

FOWLER
When other trade goods ran short, Captain Lewis exchanged his "fowling piece" for necessary supplies.

FUSILS
The fusil (often pronounced "fuzee") was a lighter-weight, elegantly decorated musket.

HORSE PISTOLS & POCKET PISTOLS
These usually came in pairs. While preparing for the journey, Captain Lewis purchased a pair of pocket pistols with secret triggers for $10.00. Horse pistols (which were larger than pocket pistols) were carried in holsters, saddlebag fashion, over the front of a saddle.

MUSKETS
Springfield Model 1795

HUNTING "KENTUCKY" RIFLES

SWIVEL CANNON & SWIVEL BLUNDERBUSSES
A swivel cannon was mounted on the bow of the keelboat; two swivel blunderbusses were mounted on the stern.

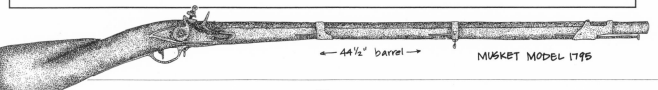

← 44½" barrel →   MUSKET MODEL 1795

The Country Through Which You'll Pass
"...eight thousand miles went the corps"

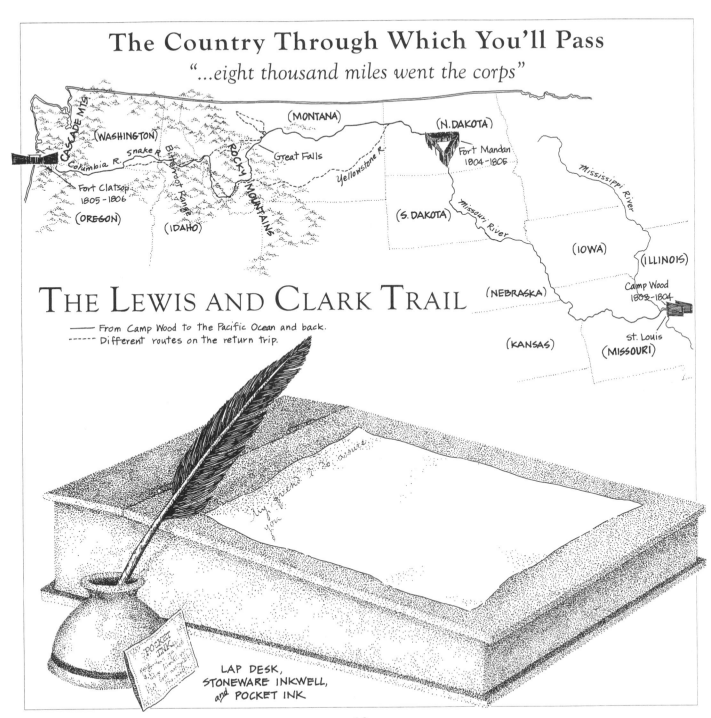

(WASHINGTON)
CASCADE MTS
Columbia R.
Snake R.
Bitterroot Range
ROCKY MOUNTAINS
(MONTANA)
Great Falls
Yellowstone R.
(N. DAKOTA)
Fort Mandan 1804-1805
Mississippi River
Fort Clatsop 1805-1806
(OREGON)
(IDAHO)
(S. DAKOTA)
Missouri River
(IOWA)
(ILLINOIS)
Camp Wood 1803-1804
(NEBRASKA)
St. Louis
(MISSOURI)
(KANSAS)

THE LEWIS AND CLARK TRAIL

—— From Camp Wood to the Pacific Ocean and back.
----- Different routes on the return trip.

LAP DESK,
STONEWARE INKWELL,
and POCKET INK

POCKET INK

19

Notes & Observations
"Three hundred new plants and animals..."

The captains filled their journals with fascinating information. They described—and sometimes illustrated—some 178 plants and 122 animals new to science. Temperature readings were recorded twice daily (until the last thermometer broke), and climatic conditions were noted. Latitude and longitude were established on a continual basis and written down for future mapmaking. The abundance of details and many anecdotal accounts contained within the journals enable the reader to experience day-to-day life on a rugged trek into unknown lands. Through the eyes of Meriwether Lewis, William Clark, and other expedition journalists, we can see our country as if for the first time and appreciate it as never before.

"communicate to us, at seasonable intervals, a copy of your journal, notes & observations of every kind"

THOMAS JEFFERSON
June 20, 1803

vivid purple-blue blooms
Apr. 14, 1806

↑ to 16" ↓

MENZIES' LARKSPUR
Delphinium menziesii

Journal Keepers

"The serg.ᵗˢ...are directed each to keep a seperate journal from day to day of all passing occurrences"

DETACHMENT ORDERS
May 26, 1804

Captain Lewis and Captain Clark both kept journals; their writings, when combined, cover every day of the expedition. The sergeants—Charles Floyd, John Ordway, Nathaniel Pryor, and Patrick Gass—were instructed to keep diaries also. At least two of the privates followed suit: Joseph Whitehouse and Robert Frazer.

OSAGE ORANGE
Maclura pomifera

1ˢᵗ new-to-science plant collected by Lewis & Clark
Mar. 26, 1804

yellowish-green, inedible fruit

"the fins next to the gills have eleven rays each....the back is of a blueish duskey colour...belly is of a silvery white....the under jaw exceeds the upper...the scales of this little fish are so small and thin that without manute inspection you would suppose they had none....I found them best when cooked in Indian stile"

WILLIAM CLARK, February 25, 1806

Also known as CANDLEFISH; so oily that, when dried, it can be strung with a wick and used as a candle.

Feb. 24, 1806

EULACHON
Thaleichthys pacificus

20

Creating the journals was no small task. Rough notes were written each day in field books, notebooks, and on loose papers, then carefully stored away to be later developed into more complete records. The result is a national treasure totaling over one million words. One of the original field books, kept in St. Louis by the Missouri Historical Society, is Captain Clark's elkskin-covered journal. Used during the last four months of 1805, this journal contains more than a dozen full-page maps in addition to daily events. The floor plan for Fort Clatsop is sketched on its cover.

"we have encouraged our men to keep journals, and seven of them do so, to whom in this respect we give every assistance in our power."

MERIWETHER LEWIS, April 7, 1805

The following buckskin-covered book makes an attractive volume for recording nature notes or keeping pressed plants.

BUCKSKIN-COVERED JOURNAL

MATERIALS:

- one $9^3/_4$-inch x 6-inch rectangle of soft, thin buckskin
- five 9-inch x $^3/_{16}$-inch buckskin thongs
- six $8^1/_2$-inch x 11-inch pieces of buff-colored cardstock
- paper hole punch, $^1/_8$-inch hole size
- yarn needle (blunt, with large eye)
- all-purpose glue

DIRECTIONS:

- Cut cardstock into quarters, creating twenty-four $4^1/_4$-inch x $5^1/_2$-inch pieces.
- On one of the pages, measure and mark for five holes, $^3/_8$-inch in from the long left edge; mark from top to bottom at $^3/_4$-inch, $1^3/_4$-inch, $2^3/_4$-inch, $3^3/_4$-inch, and $4^3/_4$-inch. Punch holes at marks.
- Using this page as a template, punch remaining pages. *Be careful to align holes and pages as closely to template as possible.*
- Stack punched pages and square up to make sure holes align. Place stack on right inner side of buckskin rectangle. Fold left side over stack and adjust as needed to center stack within cover.
- Working top to bottom, mark holes at 1-inch intervals on buckskin, $^1/_2$-inch from spine on both front and back cover. Check as you go to make sure that marks are directly over page holes. Set stack of pages aside.
- Use paper hole punch to punch holes through buckskin at marks.
- Return stack of pages to buckskin cover. Use yarn needle to carefully work a buckskin thong through top holes: first through front cover, then through the pages (a few at a time), and finally through the back cover. Knot loose ends of buckskin thong at spine.
- Repeat process (working top to bottom) with remaining pages, checking regularly for hole alignment and evenness of pages. Clip thong ends to 2 inches or desired length.
- Glue first and last page to inside of front and back cover to reinforce buckskin.

SHAWNEE

DELAWARE

KICKAPOO

SAC & FOX

OSAGE

KANSA

OTO

MISSOURI

PAWNEE

YANKTON SIOUX

TETON SIOUX

CHEYENNE

OMAHA

ARIKARA

MANDAN

HIDATSA

PLAINS CREE

ASSINIBOIN

SHOSHONI

SALISH

NEZ PERCE

YAKAMA

The Nations and Their Numbers

"many different Indian tribes..."

Lewis and Clark hoped to meet with as many American Indian nations as possible. Some would already be familiar; others—especially those whose territories lay farther to the west—would be new to the explorers. By the end of the journey, the captains had compiled information on roughly fifty different tribes, much of it the result of direct contact.

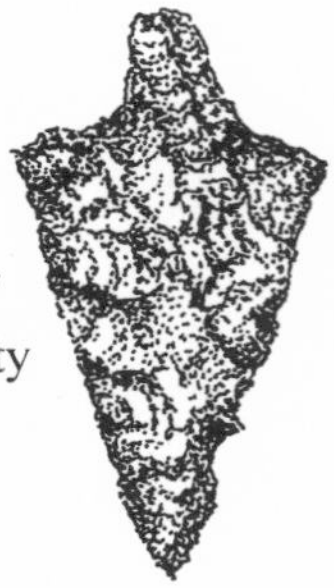

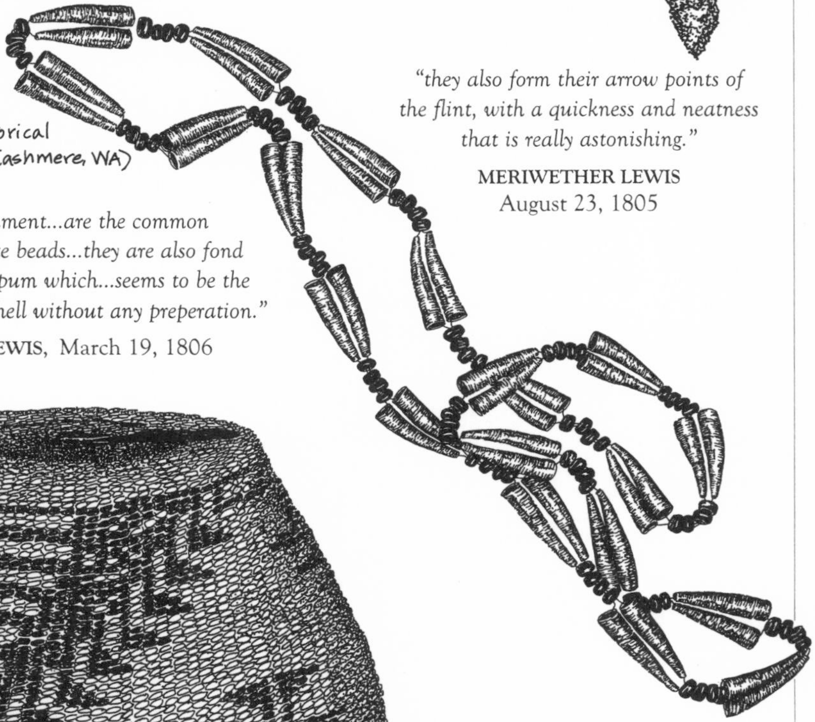

DENTALIUM
SHELL & BLUE
BEAD NECKLACE

(Chelan County Historical
Society Museum, Cashmere, WA)

"they also form their arrow points of the flint, with a quickness and neatness that is really astonishing."
MERIWETHER LEWIS
August 23, 1805

"The favorite ornament...are the common coarse blue and white beads...they are also fond of a species of wampum which...seems to be the native form of the shell without any preperation."
MERIWETHER LEWIS, March 19, 1806

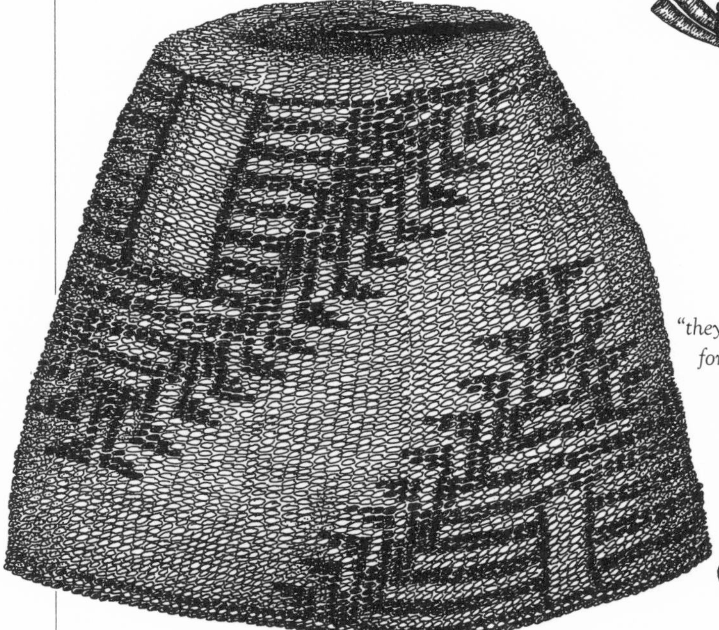

"they also wear a cap or cup on the head formed of beargrass and cedarbark."
MERIWETHER LEWIS
May 13, 1806

Nez Perce
WOMAN'S HAT
Nez Perce: LÍ·CKAẃ

(Nez Perce National Historical
Park, Spalding, ID)

Because gift giving and trade were an important part of building cross-cultural relations, the expedition carried a wide variety of goods thought to be valued by the people they would meet. Several hundred dollars' worth of items were packed away, much of it in bundles destined for particular groups. These gifts would demonstrate the friendly intentions of the expedition and encourage commerce between cultures.

HAWK BELLS

INDIAN PRESENTS

THIMBLE
Thimbles were often pierced & sewn onto clothing, etc, for decoration.

12	Pipe Tomahawks
6 $^{1}/_{2}$ ^{lbs}	Strips Sheet Iron
1	P^{s}. red flannel 47 $^{1}/_{2}$ yds
11	p^{s}. Hanckercheifs ass^{d}
1	doz. Ivory Combs
$^{1}/_{2}$	Catty Ind^{a}. S. Silk
21	^{lbs}. Tread ass^{d}
1	P^{s}. Scarlet Cloth 22 y^{ds}.
5 $^{1}/_{2}$	doz fan:^{t} Floss
6	Gro: Binding
2	Cards Beads
4	doz: Butcher Knives
12	doz. Pocket Looking Glasses
15	doz. Pewter d^{o} d^{o}
8	doz. Burning d^{o}
2	doz. Nonesopretty
2	doz. Red strip'd tapes
72	p^{s}. Strip'd silk ribbon
3	^{lbs} Beads
6	Papers Small Bells
1	box with 100 larger d^{o}.
73	Bunches Beads ass^{d}
3 $^{1}/_{2}$	doz: Tinsel Bands ass^{d}
1	doz: Needle Cases
2 $^{3}/_{4}$	doz Lockets

8 $^{1}/_{2}$ ^{lbs}	Red Beads
2	doz: Earings
8	Brass Kettles a 4/ Per lb.
12	^{lbs}. Brass Strips
500	Broaches
72	Rings
2	Corn Mills
15	doz: Scissors
12	^{lbs}. Brass Wire
14	^{lbs} Knitting Pins
4600	Needles ass^{d}.
2800	Fish Hooks ass^{d}
1	Gro: Iron Combs
3	Gro: Curtain Rings
2	Gro: Thimbles ass^{d}.
11	doz: Knives
10	^{lbs}. Brads
8	^{lbs}. Red lead
2	^{lbs}. Vermillion
130	Rolls of Tobacco (pigtail)
48	Calico Ruffled Shirts
15	Blankets (from P. Store)
1	Trunk to pack sundry Ind: Pres^{ts}
8	Groce Seat or Mockasin Awls

RINGS
with stones of "Coulour'd Glass"

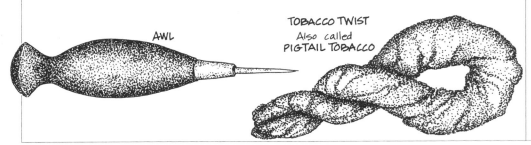

AWL

TOBACCO TWIST
Also called
PIGTAIL TOBACCO

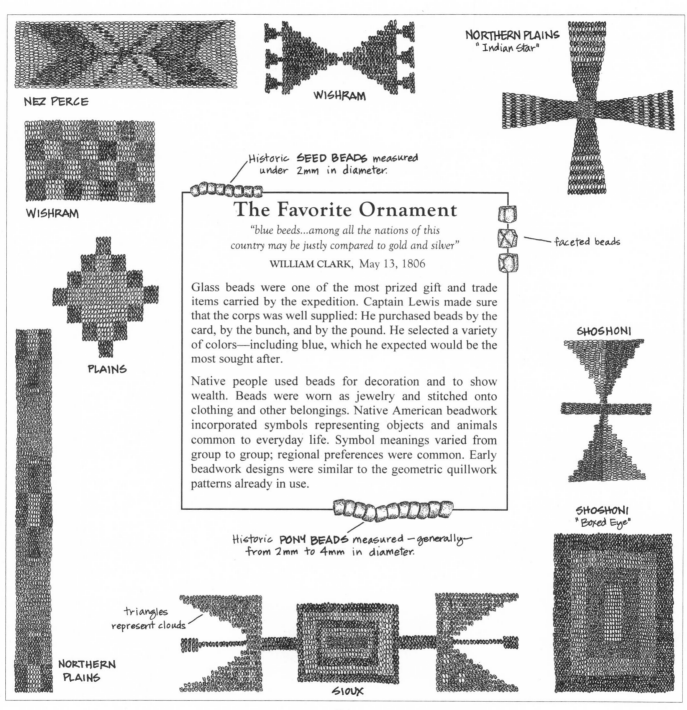

NEZ PERCE

WISHRAM

NORTHERN PLAINS
"Indian Star"

Historic **SEED BEADS** measured under 2mm in diameter.

faceted beads

The Favorite Ornament

"blue beads...among all the nations of this country may be justly compared to gold and silver"

WILLIAM CLARK, May 13, 1806

Glass beads were one of the most prized gift and trade items carried by the expedition. Captain Lewis made sure that the corps was well supplied: He purchased beads by the card, by the bunch, and by the pound. He selected a variety of colors—including blue, which he expected would be the most sought after.

Native people used beads for decoration and to show wealth. Beads were worn as jewelry and stitched onto clothing and other belongings. Native American beadwork incorporated symbols representing objects and animals common to everyday life. Symbol meanings varied from group to group; regional preferences were common. Early beadwork designs were similar to the geometric quillwork patterns already in use.

WISHRAM

PLAINS

SHOSHONI

SHOSHONI
"Boxed Eye"

Historic **PONY BEADS** measured —generally— from 2mm to 4mm in diameter.

triangles represent clouds

NORTHERN PLAINS

SIOUX

JEFFERSON'S DREAM

For at least twenty years, Thomas Jefferson had been thinking, writing, and dreaming about an exploration of the area beyond the western border of the United States, from the Mississippi River to the Pacific Ocean. President Jefferson was a man of vision and curiosity; he saw enormous potential in the land and wanted to learn everything he could about it. The purchase of the Louisiana Territory, made just prior to the expedition, gave added importance to the success of such a venture.

The President was confident in selecting Meriwether Lewis, his secretary, to lead the project. He had known Lewis for many years—both personally and professionally—and found him well qualified for the job. To equip Lewis even further, Jefferson arranged for him to train with some of the recognized experts of the day.

Jefferson's Dream

Thomas Jefferson had a dream
To explore the unknown West,
He knew that it was bound to be
A rugged, daunting quest;
The Missouri to the Rockies,
And then they'd go beyond,
To determine what this continent held
For future rising sons.

The third President had a dream
To discover many things
In science and geography,
History, ethnology;
To broaden this great land
We call America—
Mr. Jefferson had a dream.

He chose Meriwether Lewis,
A brave and prudent man,
To lead the expedition
With a firm and even hand;
To gather information
On everything they found:
The people, plants, and wildlife,
The rivers, rocks, and ground.

"Capt. Lewis is brave, prudent, habituated to the woods, & familiar with Indian manners and character. He is not regularly educated, but he possesses a great mass of accurate observation on all the subjects of nature which present themselves here, & will therefore readily select those only in his new route which shall be new. He has qualified himself for those observations of longitude & latitude necessary to fix the points of the line he will go over."

THOMAS JEFFERSON
February 28, 1803

With the Louisiana Purchase in 1803, Thomas Jefferson's administration increased the area of the United States by 827,987 square miles, nearly doubling the size of the country. This 15-million-dollar bargain (less than four cents per acre!) stretched from the Mississippi River to the Rocky Mountains and from the Canadian border to the Gulf of Mexico. It significantly increased the economic resources of the United States and opened wide the door for westward expansion.

THIMBLEBERRY
Rubus parviflorus

White "tissue paper" blooms; dull red berries.   Apr. 15, 1806

Yakama ROOT BAG

Woven and worn by women, root bags were tied to the waist while digging roots to hold the harvest.

(Yakama Nation Museum, Toppenish, WA)

↑ approx. 10" ↓

Worthy of Notice
"people, plants and wildlife..."

In a letter to Lewis, the President gave specific instructions for the exploration. He asked for painstakingly accurate maps to be made as they progressed and close attention paid to the rivers, soil, plants, wildlife, fossils, minerals, volcanoes, and climate. He also directed the explorers to become acquainted with American Indian groups as they traveled, to learn about their territories, traditions, languages, and "manners generally."

Jefferson's dream was about to come to fruition— the potential for discovery was boundless!

WESTERN RED CURRANT
Ribes cereum
June 18, 1805

translucent red berries

Mr. Jefferson

Thomas Jefferson was a man of many interests and talents. In addition to being a brilliant writer, inventor, and architect, he grew exceptional gardens and developed an extensive library of more than 1,250 books—including more books on American geography than any other library in the world. Jefferson, who once wrote that music "furnishes a delightful recreation for the hours of respite from the cares of the day," was also an accomplished violinist and enjoyed playing in chamber music concerts. His political and philosophical influence continues to be a source of inspiration for Americans today.

"you will therefore endeavor to make yourself acquainted, as far as a
diligent pursuit of your journey shall admit,

with the names of the nations & their numbers;
  the extent & limits of their possessions;
  their relations with other tribes or nations;
  their language, traditions, monuments;
  their ordinary occupations in agriculture, fishing, hunting, war, arts, &
    the implements for these;
  their food, clothing, & domestic accomodations;
  the diseases prevalent among them, & the remedies they use;
  moral & physical circumstances which distinguish them from the tribes we know;
  peculiarities in their laws, customs & dispositions;
  and articles of commerce they may need or furnish, & to what extent...."

VINE MAPLE
Acer circinatum

Described
Feb. 10, 1806

Grows in heavy
shade, damp soil.

seeds

seed wings

Fruit: double samara;
wings 1½" long & wide spreading.

"Other object worthy of notice will be
  the soil & face of the country, it's growth & vegetable productions; especially those
    not of the U.S.
  the animals of the country generally, & especially those not known in the U.S.
  the remains and accounts of any which may deemed rare or extinct;
    the mineral productions of every kind; but more particularly metals, limestone,
    pit coal & saltpetre; salines & mineral waters, noting the temperature of the
    last, & such circumstances as may indicate their character.
  Volcanic appearances.
  climate as characterized by the thermometer, by the proportion of rainy, cloudy &
    clear days, by lightening, hail, snow, ice, by the access & recess of frost, by the
    winds prevailing at different seasons, the dates at which particular plants put
    forth or lose their flowers, or leaf, times of appearance of particular birds,
    reptiles or insects."

Taken from
JEFFERSON'S INSTRUCTIONS TO LEWIS
June 20, 1803

Chestnut brown back with gray highlights;
orange belly.

DOUGLAS'S SQUIRREL
Tamiasciurus douglasii
Feb. 25, 1806

Front claws
grow 2-4" long.

GRIZZLY BEAR
CLAW

27

Meriwether Lewis was able to recognize which plants and animals were new to science because of a lifelong interest in the flora and fauna of his own country. The President arranged for him to build on that interest by studying under Dr. Benjamin Smith Barton (1766-1815), a professor of botany and author of the first textbook on botany written in the United States. Lewis's training continued as he traveled: The captains took several natural history reference books on the expedition.

Compiling a nature journal is a rewarding way to increase familiarity with what lives and grows around us. This is an ongoing activity, appropriate for all ages and skill levels.

NATURE JOURNAL

MATERIALS:
- unlined notebook or three-ring binder with blank pages (The buckskin-covered book described on page 21 makes a fine miniature nature journal.)
- pencil, ink pen, colored pencils, or watercolor paints
- magnifying glass (called "sunglass" by the captains) or jeweler's loupe
- identification guides

"Its beauty consists in a great produce of berries...literally as white as snow"

THOMAS JEFFERSON, 1813

Natural History Books Carried on the Expedition

ELEMENTS OF BOTANY, Benjamin Smith Barton (Philadelphia, 1803)

ELEMENTS OF MINERALOGY, Richard Kirwan (London, 1784; 2nd ed. 1794)

AN ILLUSTRATION OF THE SEXUAL SYSTEM OF LINNAEUS, VOL. 1 (London, 1779); and

AN ILLUSTRATION OF THE TERMINI BOTANICI OF LINNAEUS, VOL. 2 (London, 1789), John Miller

A NEW AND COMPLETE DICTIONARY OF ARTS AND SCIENCE, by a Society of Gentlemen (London, 1753; 2nd ed., 1764)

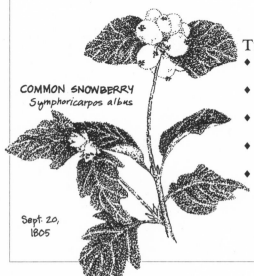

COMMON SNOWBERRY
Symphoricarpos albus

Sept. 20, 1805

TIPS ON MAKING A NATURE JOURNAL ENTRY:
- Look at your subject as closely as possible. Using magnification will enhance this process and open up new levels of study.
- Sketch your subject. Complement the drawing, if desired, with colored pencils, watercolors, or pen and ink.
- Record interesting or unusual observations; note the date and location found, plus any pertinent habitat-related findings.
- Use identification guides to verify and supplement the information you have collected.
- Becoming acquainted with common names *and* Latin binomials will add to the learning experience, as will using the correct descriptive terms for plant parts and shapes. With practice, these new vocabulary words become valuable tools for identifying and comparing your nature discoveries.

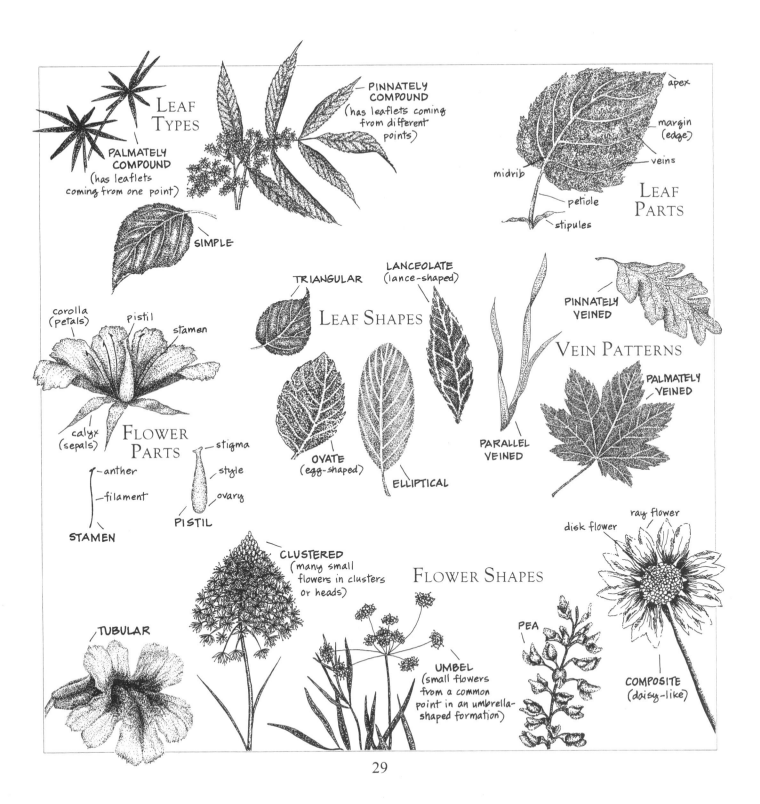

LEAF TYPES

PALMATELY COMPOUND
(has leaflets coming from one point)

PINNATELY COMPOUND
(has leaflets coming from different points)

SIMPLE

LEAF PARTS

apex
margin (edge)
veins
midrib
petiole
stipules

LEAF SHAPES

TRIANGULAR
LANCEOLATE (lance-shaped)
OVATE (egg-shaped)
ELLIPTICAL

VEIN PATTERNS

PINNATELY VEINED
PALMATELY VEINED
PARALLEL VEINED

FLOWER PARTS

corolla (petals)
pistil
stamen
calyx (sepals)

STAMEN
anther
filament

PISTIL
stigma
style
ovary

FLOWER SHAPES

TUBULAR

CLUSTERED
(many small flowers in clusters or heads)

UMBEL
(small flowers from a common point in an umbrella-shaped formation)

PEA

COMPOSITE (daisy-like)
ray flower
disk flower

29

Pressed flowers and leaves make a beautiful addition to nature journals. A plant press can be easily assembled for that purpose.

PLANT PRESS

MATERIALS:

- ◆ two 6-inch x 8-inch pine boards, at least $^1/_2$-inch thick
- ◆ four 6-inch bolts and four matching wing nuts
- ◆ corrugated cardboard
- ◆ plain white paper

DIRECTIONS:

- ◆ With boards together, drill a hole $^3/_4$-inch in from each corner. Make the holes large enough for the bolts to easily slip through.
- ◆ Cut corrugated cardboard into eight 6-inch x 8-inch pieces, clipping corners to accommodate bolts.
- ◆ Cut enough plain white paper to make two dozen 6-inch x 8-inch sheets, again clipping corners. These papers will help absorb moisture and can be replaced when soiled.

USING THE PRESS:

Carefully place plant specimens between paper sheets, then between cardboard pieces. Thicker specimens, such as daisy-type flowers, require three or four pieces of paper on either side to absorb excess moisture. Continue layering in this fashion as needed. When all specimens are situated, slip the entire "sandwich" between the two pine boards. Insert bolts and tighten down firmly with wing nuts.

It will take a week or so for the plants to dry, depending on plant type, room temperature, and humidity. Take care when removing pressed specimens; they are fragile. Glue to nature journal page, and cover, if desired, with self-adhesive laminating plastic.

lavender-blue flowers

SILKY LUPINE
Lupinus sericeus
June 5, 1806

1-3'

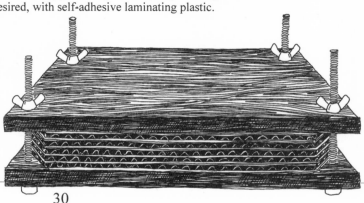

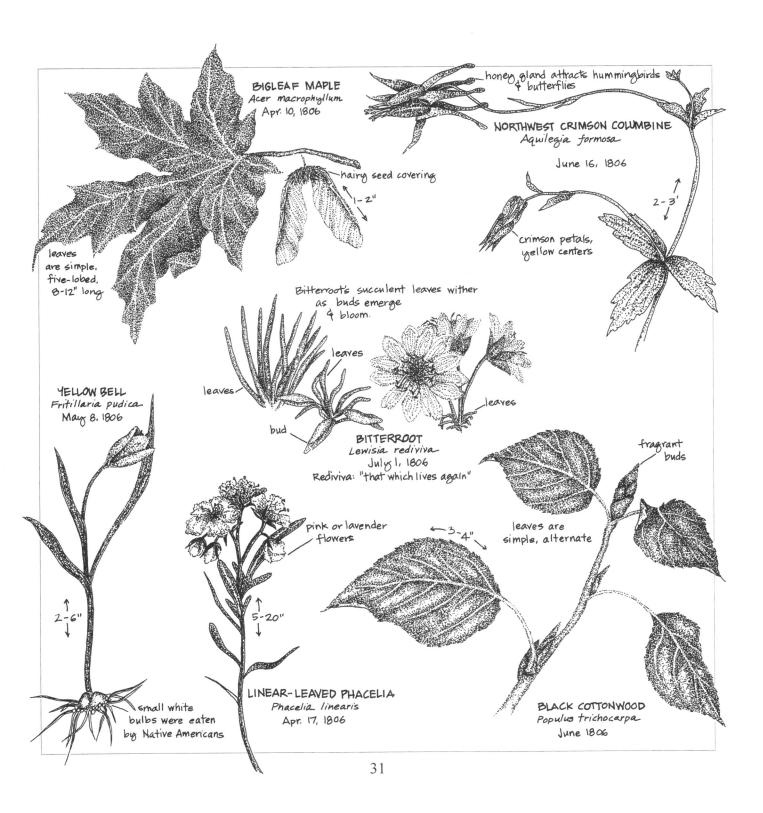

BIGLEAF MAPLE
Acer macrophyllum
Apr. 10, 1806

hairy seed covering

1-2"

leaves are simple, five-lobed, 8-12" long

honey gland attracts hummingbirds & butterflies

NORTHWEST CRIMSON COLUMBINE
Aquilegia formosa

June 16, 1806

2-3'

crimson petals, yellow centers

Bitterroot's succulent leaves wither as buds emerge & bloom.

leaves

leaves

leaves

bud

BITTERROOT
Lewisia rediviva
July 1, 1806
Rediviva: "that which lives again"

YELLOW BELL
Fritillaria pudica
May 8, 1806

2-6"

small white bulbs were eaten by Native Americans

pink or lavender flowers

5-20"

LINEAR-LEAVED PHACELIA
Phacelia linearis
Apr. 17, 1806

fragrant buds

leaves are simple, alternate

3-4"

BLACK COTTONWOOD
Populus trichocarpa
June 1806

31

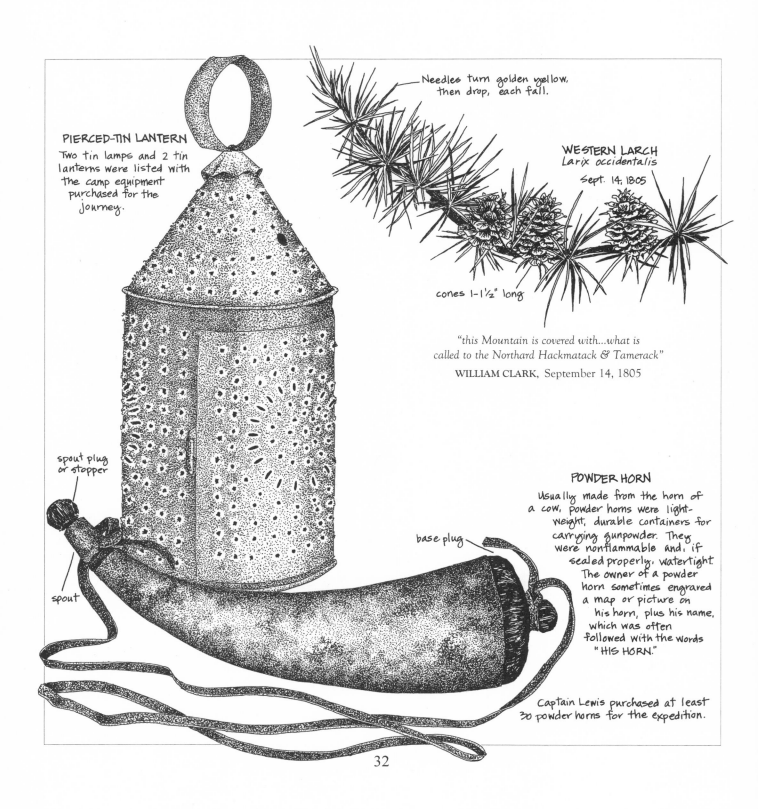

PIERCED-TIN LANTERN

Two tin lamps and 2 tin lanterns were listed with the camp equipment purchased for the journey.

Needles turn golden yellow, then drop, each fall.

WESTERN LARCH
Larix occidentalis

Sept. 14, 1805

cones 1-1½" long

"this Mountain is covered with...what is called to the Northard Hackmatack & Tamerack"

WILLIAM CLARK, September 14, 1805

spout plug or stopper

spout

base plug

POWDER HORN

Usually made from the horn of a cow, powder horns were light-weight, durable containers for carrying gunpowder. They were nonflammable and, if sealed properly, watertight. The owner of a powder horn sometimes engraved a map or picture on his horn, plus his name, which was often followed with the words "HIS HORN."

Captain Lewis purchased at least 30 powder horns for the expedition.

MERIWETHER LEWIS and WILLIAM CLARK:
UNCOMMON CAMARADERIE

During the six months that Meriwether Lewis served under William Clark in the United States Army, an abiding friendship was firmly established. It was only natural for Lewis to write to his friend several years later with an invitation to share in the adventure of a lifetime.

They had many things in common. Both were Virginia born. Both were strong, adventuresome, and loved the wilderness. They were also very different. Lewis was introspective, reserved, and socially refined. The intensive training he had received from Jefferson and members of the American Philosophical Society rendered him the better writer and naturalist. Clark, on the other hand, was pragmatic, companionable, and outgoing. He was a skilled surveyor and the better boatman.

Common strengths and beautifully balanced differences forged the strong leadership of Meriwether Lewis and William Clark. Their men responded with unwavering devotion. Remarkably, there is no record of argument—or even significant disagreement—between the captains during the twenty-eight difficult months spent together on the trail. The uncommon camaraderie enjoyed by these men built one of the greatest friendships in the history of our country.

Meriwether Lewis and William Clark: Uncommon Camaraderie

"My friend," he began, in laying out the plan
For the enterprise that he hoped they'd share;
Knowing well it would be a long, uncertain journey,
Yet there was no other man on earth with whom
The dangers he'd rather bear—

In a letter came Clark's word,
"But, my friend," he assured,
This undertaking he would like to share;
Knowing well it would be fraught with difficulties,
Yet there was no other man on earth with whom
The dangers he'd rather bear—

So arrangements were made,
The groundwork was laid,
"Co-captain" was the title they'd wear;
They knew well it would be a long, uncertain journey,
But there were no other friends on earth with whom
The dangers they'd rather share—

They had an uncommon camaraderie,
A blending of skills,
Complementing temperaments and persevering wills;
A shared spirit of adventure built this ideal team,
Capable resourcefulness and mutual esteem.

"Dear Clark...From the long and uninterrupted friendship and confidence which has subsisted between us I feel no hesitation in making to you the following communication...my plan...is to descend the Ohio in a keeled boat...thence up the Mississippi to the mouth of the Missourie, and up that river as far as it's navigation is practicable...there to prepare canoes of bark or raw-hides, and proceed to it's source, and if practicable pass over to the waters of the Columbia or Origan River and by descending it reach the Western Ocean...if therefore there is anything...in this enterprise, which would induce you to participate with me in it's fatiegues, it's dangers and it's honors, believe me there is no man on earth with whom I should feel equal pleasure in sharing them as with yourself"

MERIWETHER LEWIS
June 19, 1803

Captain Lewis's collapsible **TELESCOPE**
(Missouri Historical Society, St. Louis, MO)

← extends from 15" to 5' →

The Enterprise &c.

"...a long, uncertain journey"

"Dear Lewis...The enterprise & Mission is such as I have long anticipated & am much pleased with and as my situation in life will admit of my absence the length of time necessary to accomplish such an undertaking, I will cheerfully join you in an "official character" as mentioned in your letter and partake of all the Dangers Difficulties & fatigues...This is an imense undertaking fraited with numerous dificulties, but my friend I can assure you that no man lives with whom I would prefer to undertake and share...such a trip than yourself."

WILLIAM CLARK
July 17, 1803

The expedition was equipped with some of the best maps and accounts of the West available, including Antoine Le Page du Pratz's *The History of Louisiana* and Alexander Mackenzie's *Voyages*. The captains also carried a new map commissioned specifically for the expedition by Secretary of the Treasury Albert Gallatin.

Most of the country they would be traveling through, however, had not been mapped. They would be developing their own maps as they traveled, relying on careful observations, thorough record keeping, and information given to them by the native people who knew the land.

Mapping the Country

"Your observations are to be taken with great pains & accuracy"
THOMAS JEFFERSON, June 20, 1803

Using both celestial navigation and dead reckoning, the captains compiled daily records of courses and distances. This information allowed them to chart their progress and create maps of their route across the continent.

Celestial navigation is an accurate—but difficult—process that relies on observations of the sun, moon, stars, and planets. Dead reckoning, a method often used by the captains, involved the following steps:

- ◆ Select landmark ahead
- ◆ Take compass reading
- ◆ Estimate distance
- ◆ Travel to that point
- ◆ Backsight to repeat compass reading & distance estimate
- ◆ Record data

Depending on the situation, this process may have been completed solely through backsighting. It wasn't a flawless system, but it supplied a general idea of their whereabouts.

Clark transformed the information they had collected into remarkably accurate maps. He hadn't been formally trained in cartography, but through diligence and natural talent he proved to be a proficient mapmaker.

The Captains' Tools for
MAPMAKING & NAVIGATION

PLATTING INSTRUMENTS
TWO-POLE CHAIN
MAGNET
POCKET TELESCOPE
LOG LINE REEL & SHIP LOG
CIRCULAR PROTRACTOR & INDEX
SEXTANT
OCTANT
CHRONOMETER
COMPASSES, including a SURVEYOR'S COMPASS (also called circumferentor)
ARTIFICIAL HORIZONS (3 types), SPIRIT LEVEL, & TRIANGULAR STAND
A PRACTICAL INTRODUCTION TO SPHERICS AND NAUTICAL ASTRONOMY, Patrick Kelly (London, 1796)
THE NAUTICAL ALMANAC AND ASTRONOMICAL EPHEMERIS, the Commissioners of Longitude (London, 1781-1804)
TABLES REQUISITE TO BE USED WITH THE NAUTICAL EPHEMERIS FOR FINDING THE LATITUDE AND LONGITUDE AT SEA

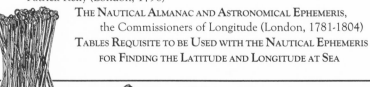

HADLEY'S QUADRANT

SEXTANT

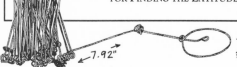

←7.92"→   TWO-POLE CHAIN
33-ft. long/ 50 links

Inestimable Friendship

"...and mutual esteem"

The mutual admiration of Lewis and Clark is easily seen in the words they used when addressing or referring to each other. "My friend." "My worthy friend." "My worthy friend and companion." All reflect a friendship that ran deep and strong. They supported one another in decision making and tenderly cared for one another in illness.

Just prior to the expedition's departure, Clark's commission arrived indicating his rank: not as captain, as they had expected, but as second lieutenant. Lewis was insistent that this information be kept between themselves and that they continue on as planned. As far as the captains were concerned, and in the minds of the expedition members, Lewis and Clark were co-commanders. When the expedition concluded, Lewis worked to see that Clark received the recognition he rightfully deserved. Lewis continued to care for the best interests of his "inestimable" friend.

"my inestimable friend and companion Cap.ᵗ Clark has also enjoyed good health generally."
MERIWETHER LEWIS
April 7, 1805

"I proceeded on...to a Point of high land distant near 20 miles. this point I have taken the Liberty of Calling after my particular friend Lewis."
WILLIAM CLARK
November 19, 1805

"I took leave of my worthy friend and companion Cap.ᵗ Clark and the party that accompanyed him. I could not avoid feeling much concern on this occasion although I hoped this seperation was only momentary."
MERIWETHER LEWIS
July 3, 1806

"my worthy friend Cap.ᵗ Lewis is recovering fast, he walked a little to day for the first time."
WILLIAM CLARK
August 22, 1806

Weighted, triangular
CHIP LOG or **LOG-SHIP**

knotted line

approx. 28"

POCKET COMPASS & CASE
Used by Captain Clark
(National Museum of American History, Smithsonian Institution, Washington, D.C.)
↑ 4" →

LOG LINE REEL
A ship's speed was measured by how many knots (on the knotted line) came off the reel in a specific amount of time. Although this method is no longer used, a ship's speed is still referred to in knots.
(The Maritime Museum, Newport News, VA)

CLARK'S NUTCRACKER
Nucifraga columbiana

Aug. 22, 1805
High mountain habitat

William Clark

William Clark was born in Caroline County, Virginia, on August 1, 1770, the ninth child in a family of ten children. His military career began at age nineteen when he signed up with the Kentucky Militia. After later joining the regular army he received repeated promotions, eventually gaining the rank of captain. Clark had retired from the army when Lewis's letter arrived inviting him to join in the transcontinental endeavor.

After the expedition, Clark was appointed superintendent of Indian affairs for the Territory of Louisiana. He married Julia Hancock in 1808 and was named governor of the Missouri Territory in 1813. Clark named his firstborn, a son, Meriwether Lewis Clark.

William Clark died in St. Louis on September 1, 1838, of natural causes.

BEAUTIFUL CLARKIA
Clarkia pulchella

Flowers have four pink, three-lobed petals.

June 1, 1806

Meriwether Lewis

Born on August 18, 1774, in Albemarle County, Virginia, Meriwether Lewis was the second child of William and Lucy Meriwether Lewis. Six months after his father's death in 1779, Lewis's mother married Captain John Marks. Together they raised Lewis and his siblings on a 1,000-acre plantation near Thomas Jefferson's home, Monticello. Lewis's mother, an herb doctor, is said to have encouraged her son in the study of plants.

In 1794, Lewis joined the U.S. Army, rising to the rank of captain by 1800. He became President Jefferson's personal secretary in early 1801, setting the stage for his role as commander of a mission to the West.

Following the expedition, Lewis was named governor of the Territory of Louisiana. During this time he was also attempting to work out details for the publication of his (and Clark's) journals. He struggled with personal and political difficulties throughout these years, leading to his apparent suicide—some believe he was murdered—on October 11, 1809.

LEWIS'S SYRINGA
Philadelphus lewisii
May 6, 1806

Idaho state flower; has fragrant, white blooms. Also known as MOCK-ORANGE.

PENKNIFE A small, single-bladed knife used to sharpen old quills and cut new ones.

To read the journals in Lewis and Clark's handwriting is a delight. The use of quill pens certainly played a part in creating the elegant style so typical of that day. Among the many items purchased for the expedition were "6 Brass Inkstands," "6 Papers Ink Powder," and "100 Quils."

Writing with a quill pen is an art. The pen's fragility and the need for repeated dipping make writing with these implements a slow process; the result, however, is lovely script.

QUILL PEN

MATERIALS:

- ◆ primary wing feather of a goose or turkey (If you are right-handed, you will be more comfortable using a left wing feather; left-handed writers should use a right wing feather.)
- ◆ bottle of writing ink
- ◆ knife or scissors for shaping tip

DIRECTIONS:

- ◆ Hardening your quill will make it last longer and perform better. To harden, simply place the quill in a sunny window for a couple of weeks.
- ◆ Prepare your quill for use by angling the end.

- ◆ Next, shape the tip to form a pointed nib. (A broad, angled nib will yield calligraphic lettering.)

- ◆ Cut a slit in the shaft.

- ◆ You may want to remove some or all of the vane from the shaft of your pen for an easier grip and to prevent the downy portion of the feather from becoming ink covered.

WRITING WITH THE QUILL PEN:

Dip pen $^1/_4$ to $^1/_2$-inch into ink. Lift pen out and gently wipe excess ink on lip of ink bottle. To write, press nib *very gently* to paper; flowing cursive strokes yield the best results.

TRAVELING INKSTAND

18ᵗʰ century design

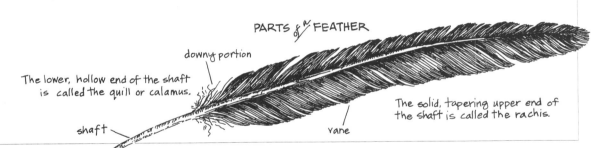

PARTS of a FEATHER

downy portion

The lower, hollow end of the shaft is called the quill or calamus.

shaft

vane

The solid, tapering upper end of the shaft is called the rachis.

37

CAMP EQUIPAGE

Purchased by Israel Whelen, Purveyor of Public Supplies, for the
Lewis and Clark Expedition to the Pacific Ocean (1803).

GIMLETS
(tools for boring holes)

shell pattern ← 5½" →

auger pattern ← 14" →

twist pattern ← 3½" →

4	Tin Horns
2	" Lanthorns
2	" Lamps
32	" Cannisters of P. Soup
1	" Box sq^r of Small ast^d
3	doz: Pint Tumblers
125	Large fish^g Hooks
	Fish^g Lines assorted
1	Stand of Fish^g d^o. with hooks Complete
1	Sportsmans flaske
8	p^s Cat gut for Mosquito Cart
6	Brass Kettles & Porterage 25 ft.
1	block tin Sauce pan
1	Corn Mill
1	Set of Gold Scales & W^{ts}
1	Rule
1	Sett Iron Weights
2	p^r Large Shears
4	doz: Pack^g. Needles & large Awls
2	doz: Table Spoons
4	drawing Knives
3	doz: Gimblets
17	d^o. files & Rasps & 1 Shoe float
1 ¼	doz. Small cord
2	Small Vices
2	p^r Plyers
1	Saw Sett
9	Chisels
2	Adzes
2	hand Saws
6	Augers 6
2	Hatchets
1	Wetstone
2	^{p}. Pocket Steel yards
	Pkg 12 lbs Castile Soap

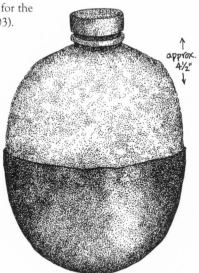

METAL FLASK used by Patrick Gass

(Lewis and Clark Interpretive Center,
Fort Canby State Park, Ilwaco, WA)

↑ approx. 4½" ↓

From Public Store.

8	Receipt Books
48	p^s Tape
6	Brass Inkstands
6	Papers Ink Powder
1	Common Tent
1	^{lb} Sealing Wax
100	Quils
1	Packing Hogshead

Bought by the Purveyor of Rich^d. Wevill

8	Tents	
45	Bags	
10	yd Country Linnen	} Oiled
20	" Brown d^o.	

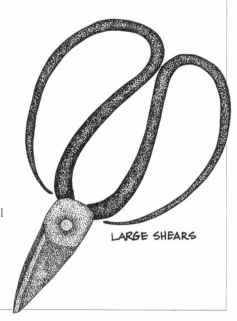

LARGE SHEARS

SEAMAN, CAPTAIN LEWIS'S DOG

The shopping list for such an excursion was huge. Meriwether Lewis spent months selecting and purchasing the many items necessary for a successful trip. Not knowing exactly how many members would be in the party—or how long they would be gone—made this critical task especially difficult.

Among other things, Lewis bought 25 axes, 400 pounds of lead, and 72 awls. He purchased powder horns, pouches, knapsacks, woolen overalls, candles, chisels, and spoons; he ordered large sheets of oiled linen that could serve as tents, boat coverings, and, if necessary, sails. For provisions the list included 3,400 pounds of flour, 3,705 pounds of pork, beans, lard, coffee, ground corn, dried apples, and sugar.

While preparing for the journey, Lewis made another important purchase: a Newfoundland dog. Appropriately named Seaman, this large, sagacious canine quickly became a prized member of the expedition.

OREGON SUNSHINE
Eriophyllum lanatum

June 6, 1806
on the Clearwater River

6-15½"

yellow flowerheads, 1½" diam.

Seaman, Captain Lewis's Dog

Seaman, a Newfoundland dog,
The captain's faithful friend—
Quite a sum was paid:
Twenty dollars he gave
To make you all his own.

Seaman, a Newfoundland dog,
The captain's faithful friend—
Active and strong,
Patrolling all the night long,
Gentle companion.

Seaman, a Newfoundland dog,
The captain's faithful friend—
Barking alarm kept the camp from harm
By bear and buffalo.

Seaman, a Newfoundland dog,
The captain's faithful friend—
Guarding the corps,
Catching beaver and squirrel,
Did you make it to the end?
Well, did you make it to the end?
Did you make it to the end?

"my dog was of the newfoundland breed very active strong and docile."
MERIWETHER LEWIS
September 11, 1803

"the dog...I prised much for his docility and qualifications generally for my journey."
MERIWETHER LEWIS
November 16, 1803

"a large buffaloe Bull...ran up the bank in full speed...when he came near the tent, my dog saved us by causing him to change his course...which he did by turning a little to the right, and was quickly out of sight"
MERIWETHER LEWIS
May 29, 1805

"The White bear...have never yet ventured to attack us and our dog gives us timely notice of their visits, he keeps constantly padroling all night."
MERIWETHER LEWIS
June 28, 1805

Sagacious
"...a Newfoundland dog"

Captain Lewis didn't record where he purchased Seaman, or exactly when. Neither did he mention why he picked a Newfoundland—but we can certainly guess. Known for its size, strength, and outstanding swimming abilities, the Newfoundland had become a popular choice of the day. Hardworking both on land and in water, Newfoundlands frequently accompanied crews on ships. The impressive capabilities of this breed, combined with intelligence and an even-tempered personality, made it a logical selection for the captain.

With webbed feet and an oily topcoat, Newfoundlands are especially suited for working in water.

"Did you make it to the end?"

We don't know whether Seaman completed the expedition. The last comment about him was recorded on July 15, 1806, when mosquitoes were tormenting both man and dog. Because Seaman was worthy of frequent mention in the journals—over thirty times—it is hard to believe that his disappearance or death would have gone unreported.

B iscuits—over 500 pounds of them—were among the food items purchased and packed away for the journey. Very unlike the fluffy breads we think of today, these biscuits were flat, hard, and bland. A time-tested staple in military cuisine, they were made simply of flour and water, then baked until thoroughly dried and nearly unbreakable. Salt was usually omitted because it would absorb moisture, which would in turn promote spoilage. Variously called hard bread, sea biscuit, ship biscuit, or pilot's bread (and in later years, hardtack), these biscuits traveled well and provided nourishment to hungry explorers, soldiers, and pioneers. One can't help but wonder if the expedition's favored canine didn't enjoy an occasional sea biscuit "treat" as well.

"we rested our selves about half an hour, and regailed ourselves on half a bisquit each and some jirks of Elk which we had taken the precaution to put in our pouches in the morning before we set out"

MERIWETHER LEWIS, September 17, 1804

Sea biscuits are *very* hard; be sure to soften your biscuits before eating by soaking them in coffee, tea, broth, or soup.

SEA BISCUITS

Combine in a bowl:

$1^1/_2$ cups unbleached flour
$^1/_2$ cup whole wheat flour
1 teaspoon salt (optional)

Add about $^3/_4$ cup water—just enough so that the mixture holds together but is not sticky. Knead until smooth. Roll out dough on floured surface to $^3/_8$-inch thickness and cut into $3^1/_2$-inch circles; a large cup works well for cutting. Pierce each biscuit several times with a toothpick. This prevents puffing, which would make the biscuits fragile and prone to breaking in storage.

Bake at 350 degrees on an ungreased cookie sheet for 30 minutes. Turn each biscuit and bake for another 20-30 minutes. Biscuits should be lightly browned.

Makes six $3^1/_2$-inch biscuits.

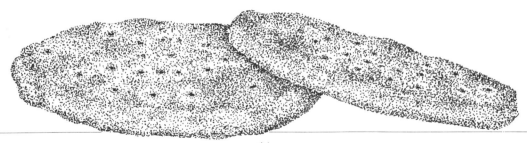

A Keeled Boat

"our provisions Goods and equipage on Board of a Boat
of 22 oars...all in health and readiness to set out.
Boats and everything Complete...for...our road across the Continent"

WILLIAM CLARK, May 13, 1804

Built to Captain Lewis's particular specifications, the keelboat measured 55 feet long by 8 feet wide. It had a 32-foot-high mast and was capable of carrying several tons of cargo. Captain Clark made beneficial modifications to the boat, including storage lockers that were placed along the sides. The lids of the lockers could be raised, if necessary, to serve as shields in case of attack.

The keelboat—or barge, as the captains called it—was taken up the Missouri using a combination of sailing (when the wind cooperated), pulling (from the riverbank with towropes called cordelles), rowing, and poling. To pole the boat upstream, each man in a group would push against the river bottom with a long pole while walking from the bow toward the stern.

DIFFICULTY, RISK, ETC.

On May 14, 1804, the Corps of Discovery left their winter camp and headed up the Missouri River "under a jentle brease." The party members were "in high Spirits" as they set sail in their fully loaded keelboat and two pirogues. Although undoubtedly aware of the dangers that lay before them, they were stouthearted and ready for the test. That fortitude was crucial: In the months ahead they would face life-threatening illness, near starvation, and debilitating fatigue. They would find themselves in treacherous situations that would require every bit of strength they could muster. Formidable obstacles would stand in their way, defying them to advance. And one of them—but only one—would perish in the endeavor.

Sketch based on Captain Clark's drawing of the keelboat. (Field notes, 1804)

Difficulty, Risk, Etc.

The corps faced many perils,
Which could have cost their lives,
Attacking beasts and illness—
Death should have been their prize;
Unrelenting exhaustion,
Sparse food to be enjoyed,
Yet the only corpsman that they lost
Was Sergeant Charlie Floyd.

Capsizing boats and snakebites,
The buffalo's stampede,
Sudden rising waters,
Unknown people that they'd meet;
Unrelenting exhaustion,
Sparse food to be enjoyed,
Yet the only corpsman that they lost
Was Sergeant Charlie Floyd.

Harsh wounds and angry grizzlies,
Storms of hail and snow,
Steep hills to climb, rugged mountains,
The raging river's tow;
Unrelenting exhaustion,
Sparse food to be enjoyed,
Yet the only corpsman that they lost
Was Sergeant Charlie Floyd.

"a large brown bear... pursued...so close that they were obliged to throw aside their guns and pouches and throw themselves into the river altho' the bank was nearly twenty feet perpendicular; so enraged was this anamal that he plunged into the river only a few feet behind"
MERIWETHER LEWIS
May 14, 1805

"the men in the water almost all day. they are geting weak soar and much fortiegued; they complained of the fortiegue to which the navigation subjected them and wished to go by land Cap: C. engouraged them and passifyed them. one of the canoes was very near overseting in a rapid today. they proceeded but slowly. at noon they had a thunderstorm which continued about half an hour."
MERIWETHER LEWIS
August 12, 1805

"with the greatest dificuelty risque &c. we made five miles 7 1/2 & Encamped"
WILLIAM CLARK
September 2, 1805

The pirogues were large canoe-shaped boats with flat bottoms and masts. One, a red craft, was manned by eight men; the other, white, carried a six-man crew.

Suffering with Hunger

"...sparse food to be enjoyed"

"most of the party is weak and feeble Suffering with hunger."

JOSEPH WHITEHOUSE
September 19, 1805

GOLDEN CURRANT
Ribes aureum
July 29, 1805

Keeping a large group of hard-working, hungry travelers fed was a considerable assignment. To accomplish the job, the party was divided into messes. "Superintendants of Provision" were appointed to each mess to receive and prepare food for the "most wholesome" and "juducious consumption." Even when game was plentiful it took a considerable quantity to appease the appetites of the men. They could consume one elk and one deer, or four deer, or one buffalo per day. If there was little or no fresh meat available, they relied on their store of provisions, on foraged plants, and on what could be purchased from local Native Americans. At times, when even these resources dwindled, the corps went hungry.

LEWIS'S LOMATIUM/BISCUITROOT
Lomatium triternatum

5-6"

May 6, 1806

Edible wild plants provided a welcome addition to the explorers' diet. Sometimes these plant foods—berries, roots, nuts, and fruit—were valued for the change they brought to otherwise monotonous meals. At other times they were relied upon as a primary food source.

Several types of berries were eaten by the corps; many were purchased from Native Americans who had picked the berries in season and dried them for later use. Yellow currants, black currants, and service berries were favorites to eat fresh. Others, including choke cherries, salal berries, and evergreen huckleberries were usually eaten dried, in the form of loaves or cakes obtained from the native people. Berries were also an ingredient in pemmican, a nourishing food made of dried berries and dried meat pounded together and mixed with melted fat.

Roots were almost always purchased from local natives who knew exactly where and what to dig. Wapato roots were a favorite of the corps; bitterroot was not. And although they found the taste of camas agreeable, it apparently did not agree with them: Nearly everyone developed a "heaviness at the stomack" after eating too freely of the roots. When wild onions were discovered growing alongside the Missouri River near Three Forks, the men took time to gather "considerable quantities" to enjoy with upcoming meals.

CALIFORNIA HAZELNUT
Corylus californica

Oct. 22, 1805

Natives along the Columbia River shared white oak acorns (which were eaten both raw and roasted) and hazelnuts with their hungry visitors. The banks of the Lower Missouri provided several types of fruit, including plums, cherries, pawpaws, and grapes.

Native Americans, frontiersmen, and settlers relied on cornmeal for sustenance when other foods were in short supply. The Lewis and Clark Expedition depended heavily on cornmeal as well: Several hundred pounds were purchased for the journey, according to Captain Clark's "Memorandum of Articles in Readiness for the Voyage."

Historical cookbooks describe a variety of items that could be made using cornmeal. Sometimes it was boiled with water and salt to create mush. Cool, firm leftovers were sliced and fried. Johnnycakes were prepared by combining water and salt with cornmeal to form a dough that was shaped into patties, then fried or baked. Because these dry cakes traveled well, they were also called "journey cakes." Corn pone and corndodgers were similar variations. When baked directly in the ashes of a campfire, these cornmeal breads were referred to as "ash cakes."

> *"Those people gave us to eate bread made of Corn"*
> **WILLIAM CLARK**, October 11, 1804

The following recipe combines cornmeal, bacon, and dried apples (all of which were packed away in the corps's larder) to make a flavorful version of a journey cake.

BACON AND DRIED APPLE CORN CAKES

Combine in saucepan:

- 2 cups cornmeal
- 3/4 teaspoon salt
- 1 cup dried apple, snipped or broken into 1/4-inch pieces
- 5 pieces fried bacon, crumbled
- 1 tablespoon sugar
- 3 cups water

Cook mixture over medium heat until thick, stirring constantly to prevent scorching. Remove from heat. Drop batter by large spoonfuls onto hot skillet that has been generously greased with bacon drippings. Flatten to form 1/2-inch-thick cakes. Fry over medium heat until bottom side is brown and crispy; turn and repeat on other side.

Serve hot with honey. Makes about 12 cakes.

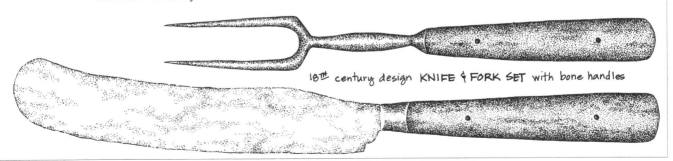

18TH century design KNIFE & FORK SET with bone handles

Several Men Taken Sick
"illness...harsh wounds..."

Although the captains were not formally trained as doctors, they were compelled to serve in that capacity on a regular basis. Lewis's skill in herbal medicine and their combined experience with frontier ailments and emergencies proved helpful in treating the medical concerns of expedition members. They sometimes served as physicians for Native Americans as well, particularly with the Nez Perce in 1806.

Prior to the expedition, Lewis received medical advice from Dr. Benjamin Rush, a signer of the Declaration of Independence and the most distinguished American physician of that time. Dr. Rush instructed Lewis in preventive and remedial medicine. He also gave guidance about which medicines to purchase, including fifty dozen purging pills known as Rush's Pills or, more colorfully, "thunderbolts."

Considering the many infirmities experienced by the Corps of Discovery, it is a credit to the captains that only one man died. Using a combination of purchased medical supplies, wild-grown remedies, and common sense, the "doctors" attentively cared for those in their charge.

Sickness on the expedition varied in size and severity. Digestive difficulties were common. Rheumatism and boils were also regular afflictions. Throughout the winter of 1805-1806 (at Fort Clatsop) many of the men complained of colds, fevers, and aches. William Bratton was so overcome with chronic back pain that Captain Lewis was "somewhat uneasy with respect to his recovery." (After months of suffering, Bratton was dramatically cured with a sweat bath treatment in which intense, moist heat was followed by a dunking in cold water.)

Numerous serious—or potentially serious—accidents and injuries occurred on the journey. Because not all of the expedition members could swim, capsizing boats were a persistent concern. Snakebites were also a frequent threat. The men slipped down precipices, suffered knife and gun wounds, and were nearly run over by a stampeding buffalo. One man rolled with his horse down a rocky creek bed; another man was almost crushed when he became trapped beneath a canoe.

"the current excessively rapid and dificuelt to assend great numbers of dangerous places, and the fatigue which we have to encounter is incretiatable the men in the water from morning untill night hauling the cord & boats walking on sharp rocks and round sliperery stones which alternately cut their feet & throw them down, notwith standing all this dificuelty they go with great chearfulness, aded to those dificuelties the rattle snakes [are] inumerable & require great caution to prevent being bitten."

WILLIAM CLARK
June 15, 1805

"we have a lame crew just now, two with tumers or bad boils on various parts of them, one with a bad stone bruise, one with his arm accedently dislocated but fortunately well replaced, and a fifth has streigned his back by sliping and falling backwards on the gunwall of the canoe."

MERIWETHER LEWIS
July 31, 1805

"Capt Lewis Still very unwell, Several men taken Sick...I administered Salts Pils Galip, [jalap] Tarter emetic &c. I feel unwell this evening"

WILLIAM CLARK
September 26, 1805

Captain Lewis's treatment for snakebite was a gunpowder & bark poultice.

NORTHERN PACIFIC RATTLER
Crotalus oreganus

Apr. 25, 1806

Deceased Brother

"...Sergeant Charlie Floyd"

A skilled Kentucky woodsman and hunter, Sergeant Charles Floyd was one of the first volunteers for service in the Corps of Discovery. He kept a daily journal from May 14, 1804, until two days before his death on August 20, 1804. The captains diagnosed his illness as "Biliose Chorlick"; some medical historians believe he died from a ruptured appendix. The best medical care of the day, had it been available, could probably not have saved him.

In March of 1857, a flood undermined the bluff where Floyd was buried and nearly took his grave with it. The gravesite was consequently moved two hundred yards east, away from the river. Sergeant Floyd's grave is now marked by a 100-foot-high white stone obelisk, completed and dedicated in 1901 by the Floyd Memorial Association. Standing tall over the Iowa prairie, it serves as a striking reminder of the young man who died while serving with the Lewis and Clark Expedition.

MEDICINE BOTTLES, TIN CANISTER & (above right) LANCET

Captain Lewis obtained over two dozen drugs to meet the medical needs of the corps, including Glauber's salt, jalap, Peruvian bark, tartar emetic, and calomel. Other medical supplies included syringes, small "pocket instruments," lancets, tin canisters, glass-stoppered bottles, and a tourniquet. Purging, bloodletting, and poultices were commonly applied medical procedures.

"I am verry Sick and Has ben for Somtime but have Recoverd my helth again"

CHARLES FLOYD
July 31, 1804

"This day Sergeant Floyd became very sick and remained so all night. He was seized with a complaint somewhat like a violent colick."

PATRICK GASS
August 15, 1804

"Sergeant Floyd much weaker and no better....no pulse & nothing will Stay a moment on his Stomach...Passed two Islands...and at the first Bluff... Serj. Floyd Died with a great deal of Composure,   before his death he Said to me, "I am going away" I want you to write me a letter."....he was buried with the Honors of War much lamented, a Seeder post...was fixed at the head of his grave. This Man at all times gave us proofs of his firmness and Determined resolution to doe Service to his Countrey and honor to himself   after paying all the honor to our Decesed brother we camped in the Mouth of floyds River about 30 yards wide, a butifull evening."

WILLIAM CLARK
August 20, 1804

"the Scioues Camps are handsom of a Conic form Covered with Buffalow Roabs Painted different colours and all compact & handsomly arranged"

WILLIAM CLARK
August 29, 1804

BUFFALO-HIDE TIPI
To create a tipi, several hides were placed over a cone-shaped frame of straight poles. The hides were fastened at the front with ties or wooden "lodge pins." Flaps at the top of these transportable dwellings allowed smoke to escape.

The captains used a "tent of dressed skins....in the Indian stile" for part of the journey. (M. Lewis, Apr. 7, 1805)

FORT MANDAN

U p the river the corps proceeded, making observations and recording all that was new. They encountered several Indian tribes: the Oto, Missouri, Yankton Sioux, Teton Sioux, and Arikara. With each tribe they held councils and attempted to establish peaceful relations. Except for a brief but tense power struggle with the Teton Sioux, most visits with the tribes went well.

Spring gave way to summer; summer, to fall. Crisp mornings urged the expedition to find a wintering ground with adequate wood, water, and game to supply their needs. Toward the end of October, they reached the villages of the Mandan and Hidatsa Indians where they were warmly received. (This area in present-day central South Dakota is referred to as the Knife River Indian Villages.) Within two weeks, near the southernmost Mandan village, they began building their winter quarters: two rows of huts joined at one end (forming an angle) with eighteen-foot-high outer walls; a connecting palisade formed the third wall. During the following five months, Fort Mandan would serve as a community hall, a busy center for trade, and a compact shelter from the extreme Northern Plains winter.

Fort Mandan

That winter a path of friendship was worn
Exchanging labor for beans and corn;
When work was done,
They brought out the horn
And fiddle for time with the Mandans.

Building their fort near an Indian tribe
Allowed them to share in a common life,
Hunting together to survive
In weather exceedingly cold.

Life was hard on the Northern Plains
Working together for food to sustain;
Most every day the Indians came
To visit and trade with the corps.

They learned of the journey that lay ahead
Through what the neighboring Indians said,
Where they would find the Missouri's head,
And mountains immensely high.

"This Morning at Daylight I went down the river with 4 men to look for a proper place to winter   proceeded down the river three miles & found a place well Supl.d with wood, & returned"

WILLIAM CLARK
November 2, 1804

"all the men at Camp Ocepied thair time dilligenently in Building their huts and got them Made comfortable...to live in."

JOSEPH WHITEHOUSE
November 2, 1804

eye

BROADAXE

15"

bit or blade

poll

helve

FELLING AXE

2½'

Many hatchets, also called tomahawks, were taken on the journey. This blade design was carried by Sgt. Patrick Gass.

(Lewis and Clark Interpretive Center, Ilwaco, WA)

HATCHET

Good Company
"a path of friendship was worn..."

Though the Fort Mandan winter had its share of hard times—particularly the bitter, lingering cold—it was a positive season for the Corps of Discovery. In a letter to his mother, Captain Lewis described the Mandans and their neighbors as "the most friendly" natives the corps had met. Indeed, the five months spent at Fort Mandan were filled with joint hunting excursions, business dealings, and shared meals. The Mandans frequently visited the fort; long hours were spent exchanging stories and trading.

During this time, the corps became a cohesive unit. Order was established. Discipline problems ceased. A family bond was created while working together in the common struggle for survival. Under the capable command of the captains and with a shared zeal for the mission ahead, they enjoyed a "perfect harmony" that would serve them well.

The captains spent the winter preparing an extensive review of the preceding months in the form of maps and reports. They looked to the future as well, questioning the Hidatsas (whose raiding parties extended to the slopes of the Rocky Mountains) about the geography and Indian population to the west.

It was a winter of reflection and preparation, of productivity and companionship.

In an Upper Missouri village, several dozen earthlodges surrounded a large open plaza. The dwellings were built by covering a framework of cottonwood logs with willow branches, followed with layers of grasses and firmly packed clay. Earthlodges lasted for several years, providing shelter for both people and horses. Bell-shaped underground storage spaces called cache pits were dug inside the lodges to hold garden produce.

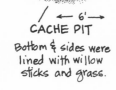

← 6' →
CACHE PIT
Bottom & sides were lined with willow sticks and grass.

EARTHLODGE,
Hidatsa: AWADI

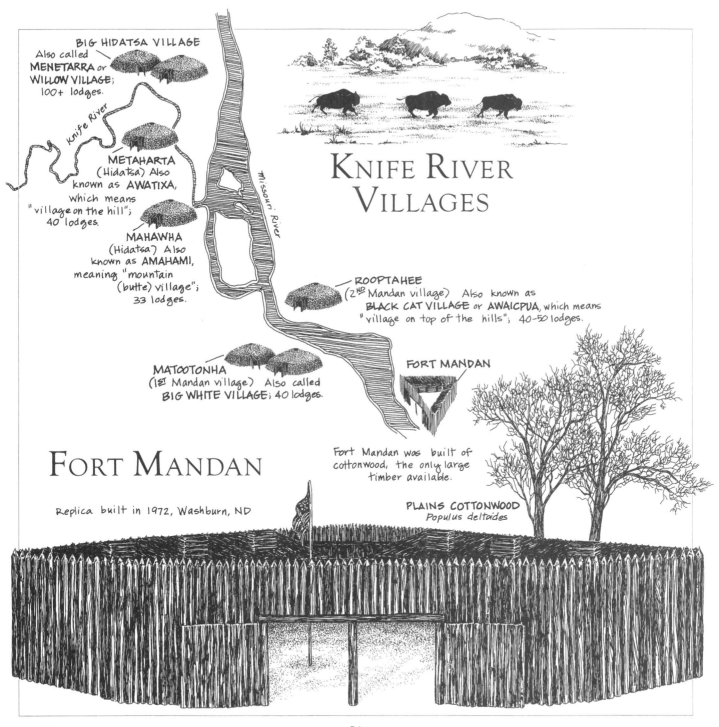

BIG HIDATSA VILLAGE
Also called **MENETARRA** or **WILLOW VILLAGE**; 100+ lodges.

Knife River

METAHARTA (Hidatsa) Also known as **AWATIXA**, which means "village on the hill"; 40 lodges.

MAHAWHA (Hidatsa) Also known as **AMAHAMI**, meaning "mountain (butte) village"; 33 lodges.

Missouri River

KNIFE RIVER VILLAGES

ROOPTAHEE (2ND Mandan village) Also known as **BLACK CAT VILLAGE** or **AWAICPUA**, which means "village on top of the hills"; 40-50 lodges.

FORT MANDAN

MATOOTONHA (1ST Mandan village) Also called **BIG WHITE VILLAGE**; 40 lodges.

Fort Mandan was built of cottonwood, the only large timber available.

PLAINS COTTONWOOD
Populus deltoïdes

FORT MANDAN

Replica built in 1972, Washburn, ND

"exchanging labor for beans and corn..."

The farming villages of the Mandan and Hidatsa served as a marketplace for trade with many groups throughout the region. Nomadic tribes traveled long distances to visit, bringing meat, leather goods, horses, and mules to trade for the valuable commodities raised by the people of the Upper Great Plains: corn, sunflowers, beans, squash, tobacco, and melons. These agricultural products were also highly valued by the Corps of Discovery. As winter progressed, corps blacksmiths were kept busy making and mending iron goods for their neighbors in exchange for food—particularly corn. Meat was often hard to come by in the extreme weather; corn pulled the corps through sparse times.

"a Great nomber of the natives men women & children visited us the whole day as we Got the Blacksmiths Shop fixed they Brought their Squaw axes & kittle to fix and mend for which they Gave us corn & beans Squasshes &C"

JOHN ORDWAY
December 29, 1804

WAR AXE

Decorated with two or more small, circular holes and attached to a 14-inch handle, this design was much in demand by the warriors of the Upper Missouri River Valley.

"a number of indians here every Day our blakSmith Mending their axes hoes &c."

WILLIAM CLARK
December 31, 1804

"a fine Day visited by Several of the Mandans to day, our Smiths are much engaged mending and makeing Axes for the Indians for which we get Corn"

WILLIAM CLARK
February 19, 1805

Family gardens of the Upper Missouri River tribes ranged from one-and-a-half acres to roughly ten acres.

The Big Four

Sunflowers were planted first, in mounds of soil called hills, around the perimeter of the garden space. Corn followed, again in hills, with seven to eight kernels per hill. Hills of squash came next. Beans were planted either among the corn, so that the vines could climb the stalks, or in hills with poles set over them to form trellises for climbing.

COMMON SUNFLOWER
Helianthus annuus

IRON HOE and "KITTLE"

BRAIDED CORN

Large or particularly well-formed ears of corn were braided into long strings (about 50 ears each) by the Mandan & Hidatsa harvesters.

The Blacksmith Shop

"the blacksmith's have proved a happy reso[r]ce to us in our present situation as I believe it would have been difficult to have devised any other method to have procured corn from the natives."

MERIWETHER LEWIS, February 6, 1805

Although several corps members were capable of blacksmithing, Private John Shields—the chief blacksmith—was especially skilled. His exceptional abilities and resourceful ingenuity were much appreciated by the captains.

Three basic tools were necessary for equipping a blacksmith shop: the forge, hammer, and anvil. Other supplementary tools included punches, chisels, files, and tongs. With a good set of tools and a supply of iron, corps blacksmiths created a variety of useful articles.

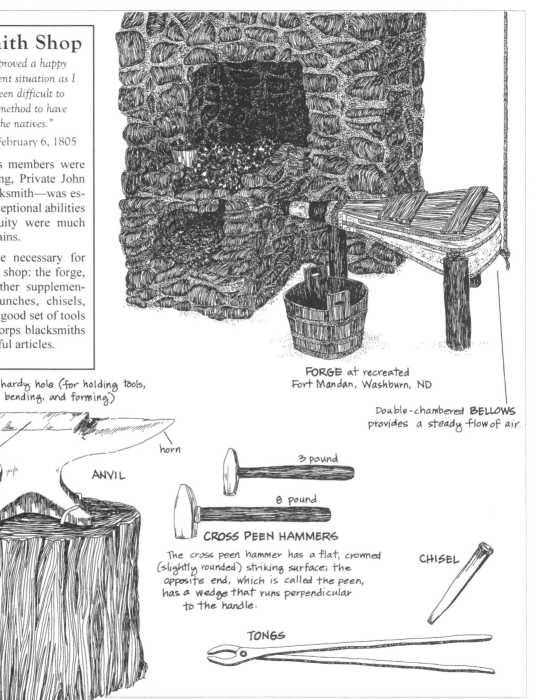

FORGE at recreated Fort Mandan, Washburn, ND

Double-chambered **BELLOWS** provides a steady flow of air.

pritchel hole (for punching and bending)

hardy hole (for holding tools, bending, and forming)

heel

face

ANVIL

horn

3 pound

8 pound

CROSS PEEN HAMMERS

The cross peen hammer has a flat, crowned (slightly rounded) striking surface; the opposite end, which is called the peen, has a wedge that runs perpendicular to the handle.

CHISEL

TONGS

framework
of willow
sticks

BURDEN BASKET

Woven exclusively by
Mandan, Hidatsa,
and Arikara women;
used to carry berries,
garden produce, fire-
wood & dirt for the
earthlodge.

(Knife River Indian Villages
National Historic Site,
Stanton, ND)

Men and women of the Upper Missouri River tribes held strictly defined roles. The men were responsible for hunting and raiding—tasks that were full of risk. Women constructed and maintained the earth-lodges, built bullboats (see page 81), planted gardens, and brought the harvest to the table.

Strips of inner
bark from ash, box elder,
or elm create the
diagonal pattern.

While collecting expedition supplies in Philadelphia, Lewis purchased three mills for grinding corn. The Mandans, who had admired the keelboat mill, were delighted to receive one from the captains. These tools, used for grinding whole corn into meal and grits, undoubtedly pleased corps cooks as well by easing food preparation.

> *"a Iron or Steel Corn Mill which we gave to the Mandins, was verry thankfully receved."*
> **WILLIAM CLARK,** October 29, 1804

Beans, squash, and corn—three of the "big four" subsistence crops of the Missouri River Valley dwellers—are combined to make this stick-to-your-ribs dish.

THREE-VEGETABLE STEW

Rinse:

    1 cup small red beans and 1 cup great northern beans. Place the beans in a large pot.

Add:

    8 cups water. Bring to a boil. Reduce heat to low.

Cover pot and simmer until tender (approximately $2\frac{1}{2}$ hours).

Add:

    $1\frac{3}{4}$ teaspoons salt

    $\frac{1}{4}$ teaspoon pepper

    2 tablespoons lard

Cover and simmer for 20 more minutes.

Add:

    4 cups cooked, cubed winter squash. Bring to a boil.

Add:

    $\frac{1}{2}$ cup corn grits. Turn heat to low and continue cooking for 5 to 10 more minutes, stirring, until grits are soft.

Makes 8 servings.

CORN
Hidatsa: **GÓOXAADI**

(Peabody Museum of Archaeology and Ethnology, Harvard University, Cambridge, MA)

Mandan yellow flint

Mandan blue

Mandan soft red flour

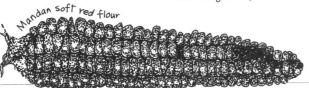

The Upper Missouri gardeners grew many varieties of corn—twenty different types have been identified—including flour corn, flint corn, sweet corn, and corn of several different colors: yellow, white, red, blue, black, pink, speckled, and spotted. Bean varieties included red pole (similar to small red kidney), shield figure, tan, and great northern. They grew several types of winter squash, some of which were similar in size, shape, and color to today's buttercup and acorn squash.

"we...went up to the 1st village of Mandans to dance as it had been their request. carried with us a fiddle & a Tambereen & a Sounden horn."

JOHN ORDWAY
January 1, 1805

Tin Blowing Trumpets

"they brought out the horn..."

The sounding horn used to celebrate with the Mandans was probably one of four horns purchased by Captain Lewis while preparing for the expedition. These "blowing trumpets" cost fifty cents each and were most likely the type used by boatmen for signaling to one another when visible identification could not be made. They were also used as calling devices while searching for lost members on the trail. Although not a true musical instrument, different tones could, with practice, be achieved.

During the Fort Mandan winter, the sounding horn served as an attention-grabbing addition to the ensemble of instruments used for merrymaking.

SOUNDING HORN
Made of tin; reed made of brass.
(Fort Clatsop National Memorial, Astoria, OR)
← 14" →

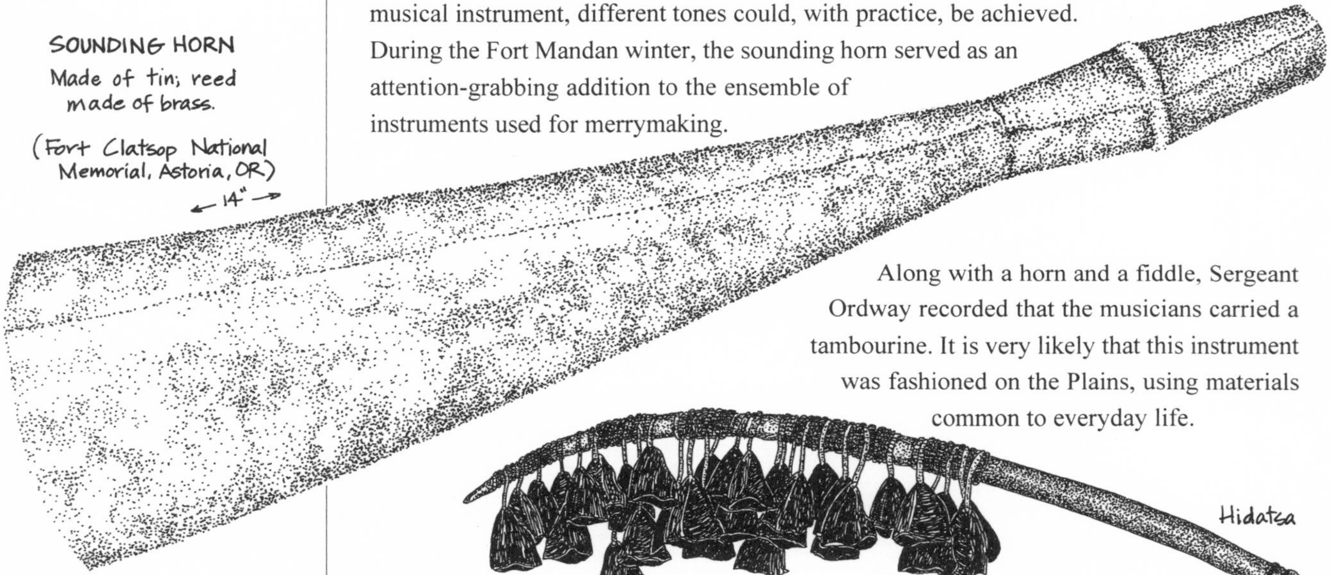

Along with a horn and a fiddle, Sergeant Ordway recorded that the musicians carried a tambourine. It is very likely that this instrument was fashioned on the Plains, using materials common to everyday life.

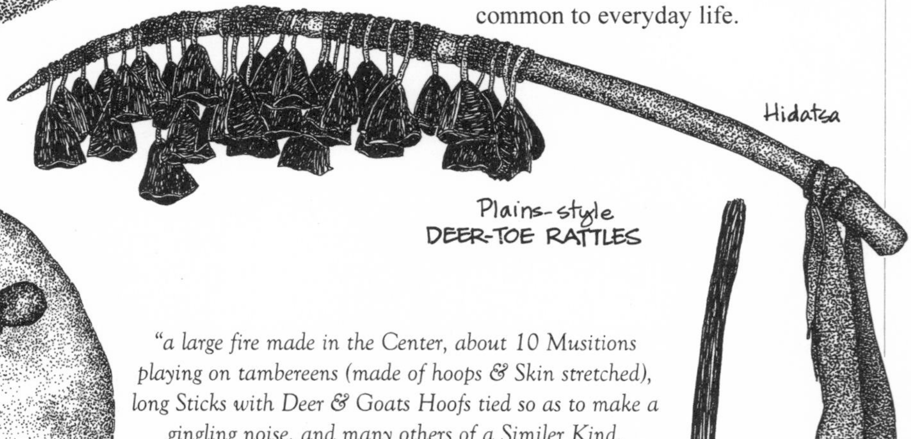

Hidatsa
Plains-style DEER-TOE RATTLES

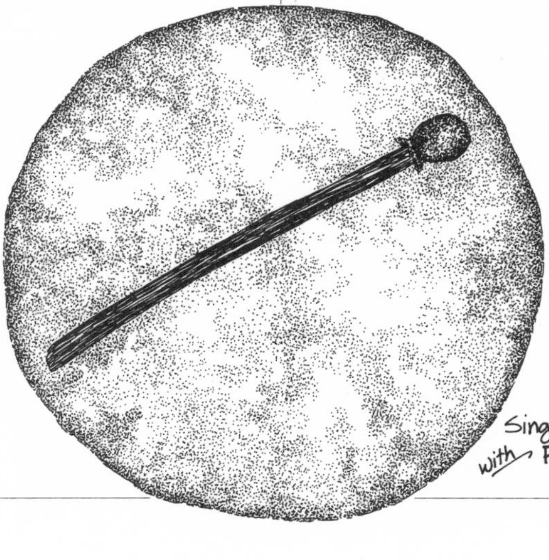

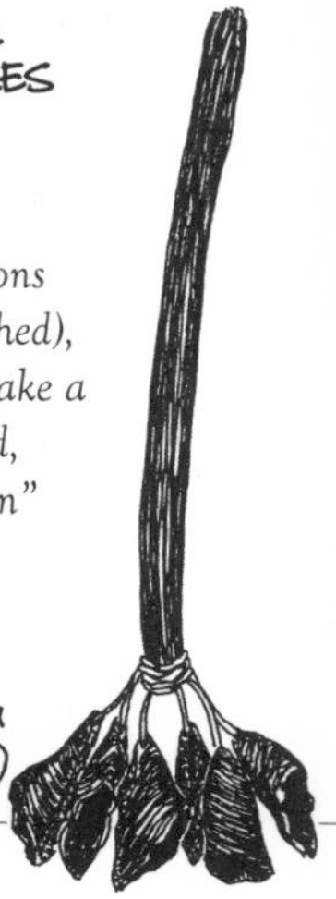

Single-headed DRUM with PADDED STICK

"a large fire made in the Center, about 10 Musitions playing on tambereens (made of hoops & Skin stretched), long Sticks with Deer & Goats Hoofs tied so as to make a gingling noise, and many others of a Similer Kind, those Men began to Sing, & Beet on the Tamboren"

WILLIAM CLARK, September 26, 1804

Arikara (AMNH)

The journalists described several different types of percussion instruments created and played by the Native American groups they encountered. Drums were constructed by stretching animal skins over wooden hoops. Rawhide pouches were filled with pebbles or small shot to make shakers. Rattles were fashioned by suspending deer and pronghorn hooves from a stick. Enjoyed by the native people during times of festive singing and dancing, these rhythm-making instruments were a curiosity to corps members.

"they all [c]ame into our Camp in the most friendly manner...Singing & playing on their curious Instruments"
JOHN ORDWAY, August 30, 1804

(AMNH)

This rattle, made with deer hooves (also called toes) and leather, produces beautiful, fluid tones.

DEER-TOE RATTLE

MATERIALS:
- twenty deer toes (available at Indian beadwork and supply stores)
- twenty 6-inch leather thongs (one for each toe)
- one 18-inch x $1^{1}/_{4}$-inch leather strap
- hand drill and $^{1}/_{8}$-inch bit
- hole punch, $^{1}/_{8}$-inch hole size

DIRECTIONS:
- Drill $^{1}/_{8}$-inch holes in deer toes, as close to tips as possible.
- Knot a leather thong at one end. Push unknotted end through hole of one of the toes, working from the inside. Pull until knot stops against the hole.
- Use punch to make a small hole at the center of the 18-inch x $1^{1}/_{4}$-inch leather strap.
- Work unknotted end of leather thong (with toe attached) through hole in strap. Tie knot on back side of strap, leaving $^{1}/_{4}$ to $^{1}/_{2}$-inch "play" between toe and strap. Trim excess thong on back side to 2 inches or desired length.
- Repeat the above process with remaining toes and thongs, punching two rows of holes $^{5}/_{8}$-inch apart, forming a cluster of toes in the middle of the strap.

TO PLAY:
Hold vertically from one end for a short staccato-type beat, or hold both ends, forming a ring, to create a flowing rhythm.

paddle
↑
approx.
9"
↓

"we are all day engaged packing up
Sundery articles to be sent to the President of the U.S....
In Box N°. 3...1 Earthen pot Such as the Mandans
manufacture and use for culinary purposes."

WILLIAM CLARK, April 3, 1805

Mandan / Hidatsa
CLAY POT and **POTTERY TOOLS**

Certain women in Mandan
& Hidatsa tribes held the
protected right to make pottery.
Coils of rolled clay were
shaped into a pot by holding
a smooth stone on the
inside of the coils while
beating the outside with
a paddle.

↑
approx.
6"
↓

(American Museum
of Natural History,
New York, NY)

← approx. →
3"

stone

SACAGAWEA

While at Fort Mandan, the captains met with Toussaint Charbonneau, a French-Canadian trader who lived among the Hidatsas and hoped to be hired by Lewis and Clark as an interpreter. His two Shoshoni wives were from an area of the Rocky Mountains near the headwaters of the Missouri. These young women had been captured several years earlier by a Hidatsa raiding party and were later married to Charbonneau. The captains agreed to hire Charbonneau.

Sacagawea, who was six months pregnant, would join the party as well. Though only in her teens, Sacagawea became a critical asset to the expedition. In addition to serving as an interpreter with the Shoshoni, she supplemented provisions by foraging for food and pointed out guiding landmarks through her home territory. Because women and children did not travel with war parties, the presence of Sacagawea and her baby brought reassurance to Native Americans who were understandably suspicious when a group of armed men approached. Sacagawea's wealth of knowledge and strong character were of considerable help to the corps.

Sacagawea

Sacagawea,
Shoshoni woman,
Though you were young you
Had seen so much life—

Taken near Three Forks
By the Hidatsas,
From them you became
Charbonneau's wife.

Helping the white men,
Sharing your language,
Teaching them things that
No one else could—

Sacagawea,
Janey, Bird Woman,
Content and determined,
Territorial guide.

"about five miles abe (above) the mouth of shell river a handsome river of about fifty yards in width discharged itself...this stream we called Sâh-câ-ger we-âh (Sah ca gah we a) or bird woman's River, after our interpreter"

MERIWETHER LEWIS
May 20, 1805

"The wife of Shabono our interpreter we find reconsiles all the Indians, as to our friendly intentions   a woman with a party of men is a token of peace"

WILLIAM CLARK
October 13, 1805

BEAVERHEAD ROCK, Montana
Shoshoni: **HA'NIIHAM BA'MBI**
↑
"about 150 feet"
↓ W. Clark

"the Indian woman recognized the point of a high plain to our right which she informed us was not very distant from the summer retreat of her nation on a river beyond the mountains which runs to the west.   this hill she says her nation calls the beaver's head"
MERIWETHER LEWIS, August 8, 1805

Of Great Service
"sharing your language...territorial guide"

Of Sacagawea's many contributions to the expedition, most important were her role in locating her homeland and her service as interpreter with the Shoshoni.

Because Sacagawea was able to remember the geography of her early years, her recognition of landmarks gave hope to travel-weary corps members. She pointed out the Three Forks area, where she was taken prisoner five years earlier, and "beaver's head," a rocky outcropping named by her people. Sacagawea's familiarity with this area proved helpful once again on the expedition's homeward journey when she advised Captain Clark on where they should pass through the mountains (present-day Bozeman Pass, Montana).

The chain of interpretation between the captains and the Shoshoni had several links: from the captains to Private Francois Labiche, who translated from English to French, then to Toussaint Charbonneau, who translated from French to Hidatsa, then finally to Sacagawea, who translated from Hidatsa to Shoshoni. A reply came back using the same process, only in reverse.

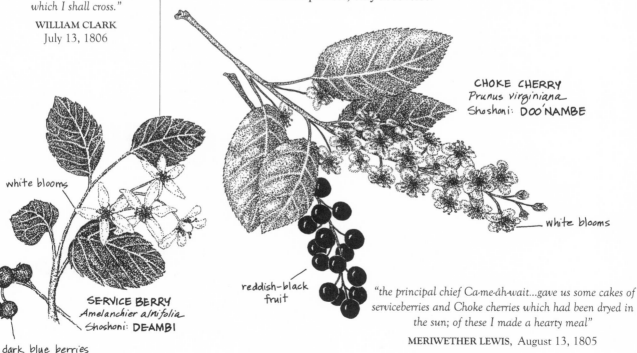

CHOKE CHERRY
Prunus virginiana
Shoshoni: DOO'NAMBE

white blooms

white blooms

reddish-black fruit

SERVICE BERRY
Amelanchier alnifolia
Shoshoni: DEAMBI

dark blue berries

"the principal chief Ca-me-âh-wait...gave us some cakes of serviceberries and Choke cherries which had been dried in the sun; of these I made a hearty meal"
MERIWETHER LEWIS, August 13, 1805

The Shoshoni were proficient at living off the land, traveling throughout their region to find seeds, roots, and edible plants in season. Sacagawea had most certainly learned in early childhood how to locate and prepare roots for food and medicine. One type of root that she brought to the corps dinner table was Jerusalem artichoke.

"when we halted for dinner the squaw busied herself in serching for the wild artichokes which the mice collect and deposit in large hoards. this operation she performed by penetrating the earth with a sharp stick about some small collections of drift wood. her labour soon proved successful, and she procured a good quantity of these roots."

MERIWETHER LEWIS, April 9, 1805

A member of the sunflower family, Jerusalem artichokes are native to North America. You may find Jerusalem artichoke tubers under the name "sunchokes" in the produce section of major grocery stores. They taste somewhat like a potato, but are mildly sweet.

FRIED JERUSALEM ARTICHOKES

Peel artichokes and slice into $^1/_8$-inch-thick disks. Fry until lightly browned in a small amount of lard. Serve toasty warm with salt.

Jerusalem artichokes may also be prepared by boiling until tender—
10 to 20 minutes, depending on the size of the tuber.
They are delicious raw as well; simply peel and enjoy.

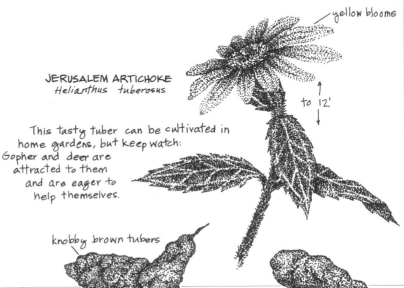

yellow blooms

JERUSALEM ARTICHOKE
Helianthus tuberosus

to 12'

DIGGING STICK
Shoshoni: **BOODO**

Roughly 3½ feet long, these sharp sticks were used for prying up roots. They often had handles fashioned from deer or elk antler.

This tasty tuber can be cultivated in home gardens, but keep watch: Gopher and deer are attracted to them and are eager to help themselves.

knobby brown tubers

— fire-hardened point

Equal Fortitude
"content and determined..."

There are several things about Sacagawea that students of history debate. One is the pronunciation of her name. "Sacajawea" is used by some groups, particularly in the West, while "Sakakawea" is favored in North Dakota. Still others feel that "Sacagawea" is the correct pronunciation.

In the process of recording Native American vocabularies, the captains took care to spell phonetically. When recording Sacagawea's name, they were consistent in using a hard "g" on the third syllable. This pronunciation means "bird woman," which is also consistent with journal documentation. (Another name used when referring to Sacagawea was the nickname "Janey," recorded by Captain Clark on two occasions.)

While the spelling of her name varies, there is little disagreement about her character. She was described as a good woman, gentle but resolute, demonstrating fortitude in the face of peril. She was attentive, content, and eager to be of service.

Jean Baptiste Charbonneau
"about five Oclock this evening one of the wives of Charbono was delivered of a fine boy."
MERIWETHER LEWIS, February 11, 1805

Jean Baptiste Charbonneau was born on February 11, 1805, to Sacagawea and Toussaint Charbonneau. This youngest member of the Lewis and Clark Expedition, nicknamed "Pomp" and "Pompy," became a favorite of Captain Clark. When the corps returned to the Mandan and Hidatsa villages in August 1806, Clark demonstrated his deep affection for the boy (now one-and-a-half years old) by offering to raise him. Because Jean Baptiste was not yet weaned, his parents declined the offer but were willing to bring him to Clark at a future date. Six years later, Jean Baptiste was left in Clark's care in St. Louis where his education commenced.

Jean Baptiste's adult life is an intriguing blend of high culture and rugged frontier. At the age of eighteen, he accompanied Prince Paul Wilhelm of Wurttemberg, Germany, to Europe. After six years in the aristocratic world of the prince, Jean Baptiste returned to America fluent in German, French, Spanish, and English. He journeyed to the West once again to live the life of a frontiersman—scouting, exploring, hunting, and serving as a guide. He died of pneumonia in Danner, Oregon, at sixty-one years of age.

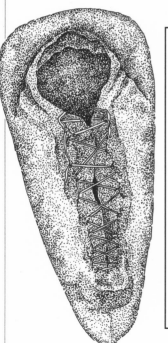

Shoshoni-style **CRADLEBOARD**
Shoshoni: **GO'HNO**
Constructed by covering a wooden frame with buckskin; used to keep infants safe & warm.

Side-seam **MOCCASINS**
Shoshoni: **BIGA NAMBE** (women's footwear)
Style common to Plains & Mountain tribes.

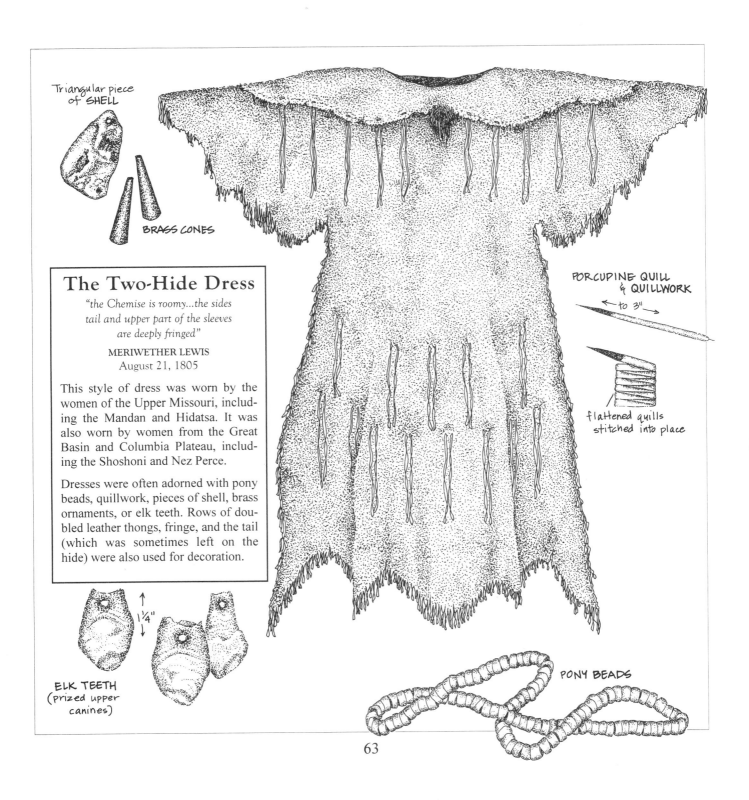

Triangular piece of SHELL

BRASS CONES

PORCUPINE QUILL & QUILLWORK

← to 3" →

flattened quills stitched into place

The Two-Hide Dress

"the Chemise is roomy...the sides tail and upper part of the sleeves are deeply fringed"

MERIWETHER LEWIS
August 21, 1805

This style of dress was worn by the women of the Upper Missouri, including the Mandan and Hidatsa. It was also worn by women from the Great Basin and Columbia Plateau, including the Shoshoni and Nez Perce.

Dresses were often adorned with pony beads, quillwork, pieces of shell, brass ornaments, or elk teeth. Rows of doubled leather thongs, fringe, and the tail (which was sometimes left on the hide) were also used for decoration.

↑ 1¼" ↓

ELK TEETH (prized upper canines)

PONY BEADS

On April 7, 1805, the keelboat left Fort Mandan under the command of Corporal Richard Warfington to return to St. Louis. It was loaded with an abundance of information for Thomas Jefferson: specimens of plants, animals, and minerals; detailed reports; Clark's map of the area they had covered thus far; and several Indian artifacts and products. Also included were six live animals: four black-billed magpies, a prairie dog, and a prairie sharp-tailed grouse. (Amazingly, the prairie dog and one hardy magpie survived the long trip from Fort Mandan to the City of Washington.)

The captains and the permanent party went the other direction, continuing their ascent of the river in the pirogues and six dugout canoes. They were zealous and ready for the challenges that lay between them and the headwaters of the Missouri. In the months to come they would struggle with a dilemma over which fork of the river to take, confront a grueling portage around the Great Falls of the Missouri, and undergo a desperate search for Sacagawea's people, the Lemhi Shoshoni.

Articles Forwarded from Fort Mandan to the President of the United States

Boxes

Skins of the Male and female Antelope, with their Skeletons.
2 Horns and ears, of the Blacktail, or Mule Deer.
A Martin Skin containing the Skin of a weasel and three Small squirels of the
    Rocky Mountains & the tail of a Mule deer fully grown.
Skeletons of the Small, or burrowing wolf of the Praries,
    the Skin haveing been lost by accedent.
2 Skeletons of the White Hair.
A Mandan bow with a quiver of Arrows the quiver containing
    Some Seed of the Mandan tobacco.
A carrot of Ricara tobacco.
4 Buffalow Robes and an ear of Mandan corn.
Skins of the Male and female Antelope, with their Skeletons
    and the Skin of a brown, or Yellow Bear.
Specimens of earths, Salts, and minerals, numbered from 1 to 67.
Specimens of plants numbered from 1 to 60.
1 earthen pot, Such as the Mandans manufacture, and use for culinary purposes.
1 tin box containing insects, mice &c
a Specimen of the fur of the Antilope.
a Specimen of a plant, and a parsel of its roots,
    highly prized by the natives as an efficatious remidy in
    the cure of the bite of the rattle snake, or Mad dog.

Large Trunks

Skins of a Male and female Braro, or burrowing Dog of the Praries, with
    the Skeleton of the female.
1 Skin of a red fox containing a Magpie.
2 Cased Skins of the white hare.
1 Minitarre Buffalow robe, containing Some articles of Indian dress.
1 Mandan Buffalow robe, containing a dressed Skin of the Lousiv[ir]e and two
    cased Skins of the burrowing Squirels of the praries
        13 red fox skins
        4 horns of the mountain ram, or big horn
        1 Buffalow robe painted by a Mandan
        man representing a battle which was
        fought 8 years since, by the Sioux &
        Ricaras, against the Mandans,
        Minitarras & Ahwahharways

Cages

Containing four liveing Magpies.
Containing a liveing burrowing Squirel of the praries.
Containing one liveing hen of the Prarie.

— 1 large par of Elk's horns connected by the frontal bone.

BLACK-BILLED MAGPIE
Pica pica hudsonia
Sept. 16, 1804

17½–22"

CRUZATTE'S FIDDLE

Music has the ability to calm raging souls and cheer the downhearted. It can bind hearts, give courage to the faint, and sooth weary minds. How fortunate it was for the Corps of Discovery to have ready access to music as they traveled. Pierre Cruzatte, who was half-French and half-Omaha Indian, was the principal musician; his exuberant fiddle playing delighted fellow corps members and Native Americans alike. The journals record over two dozen instances of musical recreation, including fiddle playing, singing, and dancing. Because there is no record of the specific songs they enjoyed, we can only look at what was popular in that day and speculate. Whatever the tunes— be they of British, Irish, or French tradition; lively jigs, patriotic choruses, or rousing hymns— we know that music played a vital role in the everyday life of the corps.

"such as were able to shake a foot amused themselves in dancing on the green to the music of the violin which Cruzatte plays extreemly well."
MERIWETHER LEWIS
June 25, 1805

Pvt. George Gibson played the violin on occasion, too.

Cruzatte's Fiddle

When the men were down,
Or had nothing to do,
Or after laboring
The whole day through,
In many situations,
Didn't matter where at,
They were brightened by the fiddle
Of Pierre Cruzatte.

They would dance a little jig
To chase away the blues,
And sing for the Indians
To delight and amuse;
In many situations,
Didn't matter where at,
They were brightened by the fiddle
Of Pierre Cruzatte.

It's really quite amazing,
Yet the story's told as true,
That the private's fine fiddle
Made it safely through;
In many situations,
Didn't matter where at,
They were brightened by the fiddle
Of Pierre Cruzatte.

The Fiddle was Played

"in many situations..."

Cruzatte's fiddle and the men's spirited dancing were a source of amusement to the native people they met along the way. Requests for demonstrations of song and dance came regularly; corps members were happy to share their merry repertoire. Many times the Indians would give a presentation of their own in return, and on at least one occasion some of the expedition members joined in, much to the delight of their native hosts. The fiddle served as a diplomatic tool as well, by calming jangled nerves and creating a cheerful atmosphere in the midst of tense relations.

Lonely nights on the trail were brightened with musical entertainment. Because singing and dancing were both favorite pastimes in that era, the corpsmen were undoubtedly well equipped with a wide variety of dance styles representing their different ethnic and geographic backgrounds. Campfire frolics provided a welcome distraction during periods of stress, a diversion to the monotony of travel. Not surprisingly, holidays were often marked with music—sometimes a full-blown celebration, sometimes a simple, single song.

"The two Chiefs much pleased with ther treatment & the Cherefullness of the party, who Danced to amuse them"

WILLIAM CLARK
November 27, 1804

"the fiddle was plyed and they danced very merrily untill 9 in the evening when a heavy shower of rain put an end to that part of the amusement tho' they continued their mirth with songs and festive jokes and were extreemly merry untill late at night."

MERIWETHER LEWIS
July 4, 1805

"a little before sun set the Chimnahpoms arrived; they were about 100 men and a fiew women; they joined the Wallahwallahs...and formed a half circle arround our camp where they waited verry patiently to see our party dance. the fiddle was played and the men amused themselves with danceing...we then requested the Indians to dance which they very chearfully complyed with; they continued their dance untill 10 at night....Some of the men who were esteemed most brave entered the space...and danced ...they were much gratified in seeing some of our party join them in their dance."

WILLIAM CLARK
April 28, 1806

SOLDIER'S JOY

magenta blooms, 1-2" long

1-2'

LEWIS'S
MONKEY FLOWER
Mimulus lewisii

POPULAR TUNES OF THE DAY

The Rose Tree
Soldiers Joy
The Irish Washerwoman
The Girl I Left Behind Me
Haste to the Wedding
The White Cockade
Fisher's Hornpipe
Coronation
Yankee Doodle
Over the Hills and Far Away
Black-eyed Susie
Chester
Rickett's Hornpipe
Over the River to Charlie
Cuckoo's Nest
Flowers of Edinburgh

A fiddle was probably not the only instrument played around evening campfires. Jew's harps were among the items brought along as gifts for Native Americans; they were very likely enjoyed by corps members as well.

"They received them verry thankfully divided them out among themselves,
& play on their juze harps, Sung &c."

JOSEPH WHITEHOUSE, August 30, 1804

Also known as jaw harp, folk harp, and trump, these portable little instruments have been used for hundreds of years by many cultures around the world. So popular were they in Europe that concertos were written for them by Austrian composer Johann Georg Albrechtsberger (1736-1809) who, incidentally, was one of Beethoven's music teachers. Jew's harps were also enjoyed by North American colonists and became a common item for trade with Native Americans.

THE JEW'S HARP

The jew's harp consists of a metal frame with a tempered steel reed. The reed, which lies between the arms of the frame, is plucked with the forefinger, causing it to vibrate. These vibrations resonate in the mouth cavity, creating the distinctive tones of the jew's harp. Once basic playing techniques are mastered, this diminutive folk instrument is great fun to play.

Above and above left: approx. actual size **FOLK HARPS** (with reeds missing) from the early 1800s. These were recovered in archeological diggings at Fort Vancouver National Historic Site, Vancouver, WA.

TO PLAY:

- Hold round end of harp with one hand, taking care to touch only the frame, not the reed.
- Bring chin forward so that upper front teeth are directly over lower front teeth. Open mouth so that front teeth are spread about $1/2$-inch apart. **This gap must be maintained while playing** to allow the reed room to vibrate **and to keep reed from hitting teeth**.
- Place arms of harp against front of teeth. Lips should rest on top and bottom of arms.
- With the other hand, strum the harp by plucking the trigger with either a pushing or pulling motion. To create volume, inhale or exhale small amounts of air.
- Practice mouthing the vowels ("A-E-I-O-U") to achieve a variety of sounds.
- Different tones are produced by changing the position of the tongue, thus altering the size of the mouth cavity. **Keep tip of tongue out of the way of the reed.**

Ornate harp on exhibit at Fort Clatsop National Memorial, Astoria, OR.

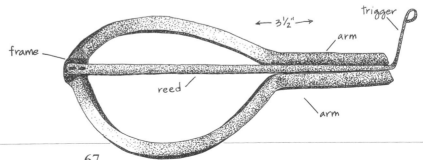

frame — reed — arm — trigger — arm — 3½"

A lthough their days were full of labor and spare time was generally rare, the corps did enjoy a few nonmusical recreational activities. During their first winter (at Camp Wood) they participated in competitive target practice. The following winter Captain Lewis reported that they played the "good old game" of backgammon. One Independence Day was celebrated with festive joke telling; other holidays were marked with a shout, a salute, and a discharge of guns and cannons. Many in the party, including Sacagawea, fished for pleasure as well as out of necessity—especially Silas Goodrich, who was "remarkably fond of fishing." Some enjoyed collecting souvenirs as they traveled; on-the-trail entertainment would most certainly have been provided by Seaman as well. And at least one other animal amused the men for a time: George Drouillard caught a young beaver and kept it as a pet.

While waiting for the deep mountain snowpack to diminish on their 1806 return trip, they passed time by running foot races with the Nez Perce—one of whom proved "as fleet as Drewyer [Drouillard] and R. Fields, our swiftest runners." Here they also pitched quoits (a game similar to horseshoes) and played an old version of tag called prisoner's base.

"when the racing was over the men divided themselves into two parties and played prison base"

MERIWETHER LEWIS, June 8, 1806

PRISONER'S BASE

Two teams, equal in number, form lines facing each other twenty to thirty yards apart, creating a playing field. Each team designates two areas: one for a prison and another for home base. (Colored armbands help distinguish one team from another.)

To begin the game, one player leaves his team (team A) and runs onto the playing field, daring his opponents. A player from the opposite team (team B) gives chase, attempting to tag the first player before he can return to home base, where players are considered safe. A second player from team A issues out in pursuit of the opponent giving chase, followed by yet another pursuer from team B, and so forth, until all players have joined the game, each pursuing and each being pursued. If a player is tagged, he goes to the opposing team's prison where he can be freed only by the touch of a teammate; the player who tagged him races back to home base and prepares to chase another opponent.

The team that manages to keep all opponents in prison at the same time wins the game.

C orps members also enjoyed recreation as spectators. Captain Lewis described a game played by Northwest Coast tribes that involved bowling a small playing piece between two upright sticks. The journals tell of another game played by Northwest Coast, Hidatsa, and Shoshoni tribes that began with a player hiding a bean-sized object in one of his hands. With an accompanying song in the background, his competitors tried to guess which hand held the object. During the 1804-1805 winter, Sergeant Ordway watched a group of Mandan men play a field sport. In this game, called *tchung-kee*, a polished stone with a hole in the center was rolled down a smooth, fifty-yard-long playing area. Two competing players, running side by side, would throw long poles in an attempt to spear the stone.

TCHUNG-KEE STONE

(Knife River Indian Villages, Stanton, ND)

BITTERROOT MOUNTAINS

After locating the Shoshoni and purchasing horses necessary for crossing the Rockies, the expedition pressed on through some of the most rugged country they had seen thus far. On September 4, 1805, they descended from steep hillsides to a valley of roots and herbs. Here they met a large band of friendly Salish (Flathead) Indians from whom they bought eleven additional "ellegant" horses. Having extra horses would soon be crucial: The Bitterroots, described by Sergeant Patrick Gass as "the most terrible mountains I ever beheld," loomed to the west.

After pausing for a day by a creek they named Traveler's Rest, they began what many consider to be the most arduous portion of the entire journey. The trail they would be following was a treacherous, seemingly endless path that tested the corps to the very edge of endurance.

BITTERROOT
Lewisia rediviva

fleshy taproot

Montana State flower; grows 1-3" tall & has delicate pink blooms.

"had a very bitter taste"
MERIWETHER LEWIS
August 22, 1805

Bitterroot Mountains

Making their way
O'er the Bitterroot Mountains,
Following an old Indian trail;
Determined to pass through these
Evergreen mountains
In spite of snow, rain, and hail.

Wet and cold as never before,
Fatigue and hunger went with the corps,
As they struggled
Eleven long days to cross o'er
Those rugged, winding mountains.

Game became scarce,
And with meager provisions
They were desperate
For food to be found;
Hillsides steep
Threatened certain destruction
If horse or traveler fell down.

There was much joy
When off in the distance
An immense prairie land came in sight;
Soon they met up with the
Nez Perce Indians—
What a triumph in camp that night,
What a triumph in camp that night.

"From this mountain I could observe high ruged mountains in every direction as far as I could see."
WILLIAM CLARK
September 15, 1805

"when we awoke this morning to our great Surprise we were covred with Snow which had fallen about 2 Inches the latter part of last night...Some of the men without Socks raped rags on their feet, and loaded up our horses and Set out without anything to eat, and proceeded on. could hardly See the old trail for the Snow."
JOSEPH WHITEHOUSE
September 16, 1805

"I have been wet and as cold in every part as I ever was in my life, indeed I was...fearfull my feet would freeze in the thin Mockirsons which I wore"
WILLIAM CLARK
September 16, 1805

"obliged...to pass on the sides of rocks where one false step of a horse would be certain destruction."
WILLIAM CLARK
September 19, 1805

"continued on & passed Some most intolerable road on the Sides of the Steep Stoney mountains"

WILLIAM CLARK
September 12, 1805

"the road was excessively dangerous...being a narrow rockey path generally on the side of [a] steep precipice, from which in many places if e[i]ther man or horse were precipitated they would inevitably be dashed in pieces."

MERIWETHER LEWIS
September 19, 1805

A Most Intolerable Road
"following an old Indian trail..."

The trail over the Bitterroot Mountains had been used for generations by the Nez Perce, traveling east to hunt buffalo and to trade with the people of the Plains. They called the route "k̓useyneʔískit" or "Road to Buffalo Country." The Salish followed this path as well, traveling west to visit the Nez Perce and to places beyond where they traded with the Plateau and Northwest Coast Indians. Heavily timbered, rocky and steep, this trail was a challenge for those who knew it well. For the Lewis and Clark Expedition—unfamiliar with the terrain and with no map to follow—the challenge was multiplied.

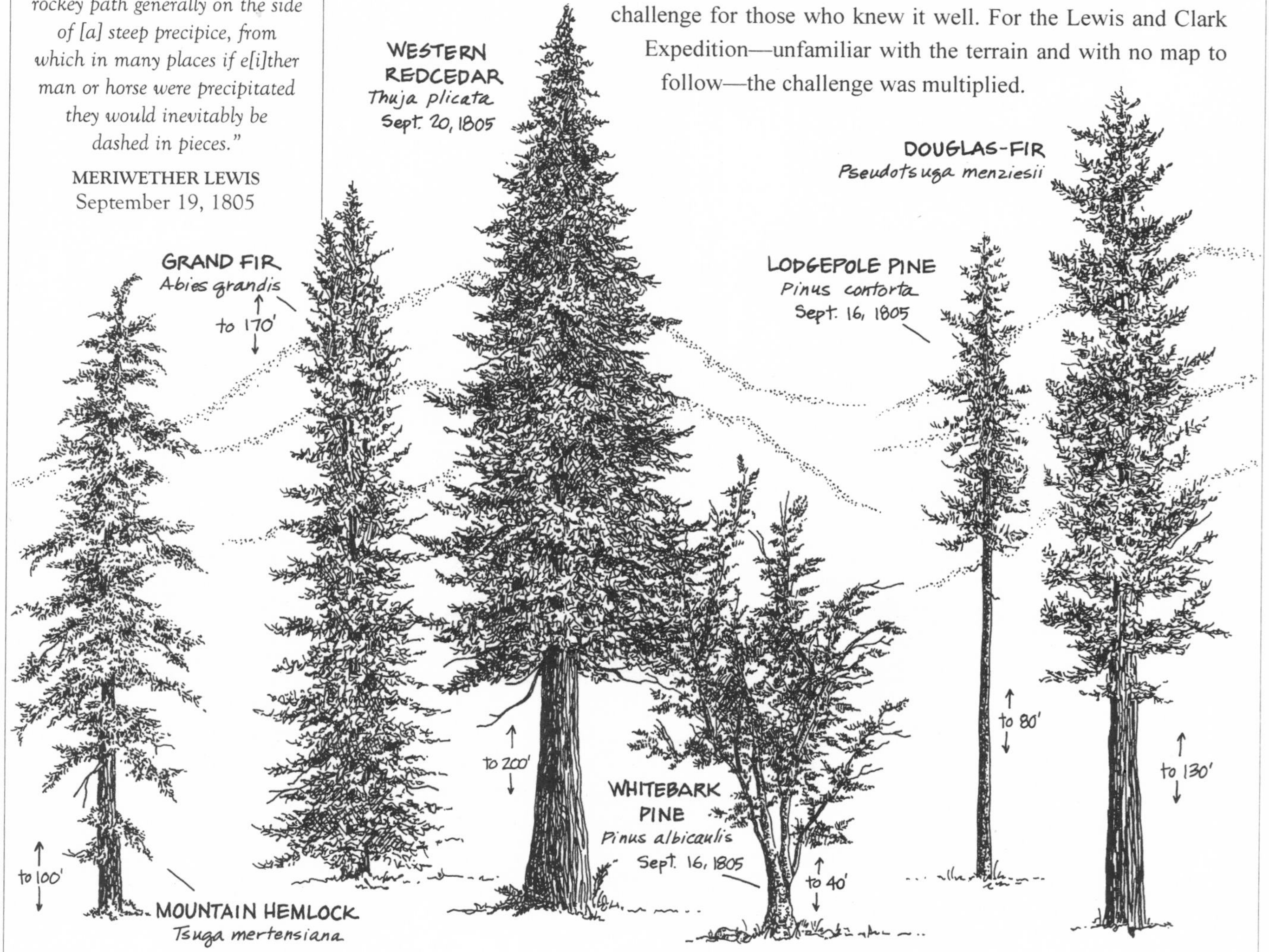

WESTERN
REDCEDAR
Thuja plicata
Sept. 20, 1805

DOUGLAS-FIR
Pseudotsuga menziesii

GRAND FIR
Abies grandis
to 170'

LODGEPOLE PINE
Pinus contorta
Sept. 16, 1805

to 200'

to 80'

to 130'

WHITEBARK
PINE
Pinus albicaulis
Sept. 16, 1805

to 40'

to 100'

MOUNTAIN HEMLOCK
Tsuga mertensiana

Because of the difficult circumstances under which they were traveling, the captains were probably unable to fully appreciate the magnificent beauty of the Bitterroots. They did take time, however, to make scientific observations along the way, noting several species of birds and evergreen trees. Emerald-clad mountainsides and deep river valleys create a majestic scene for today's traveler that is in many places very much the same as it appeared to Lewis and Clark.

EVERGREENS OF THE BITTERROOTS

"discover 8 distinct kinds of pine on those mountains"
WILLIAM CLARK, September 16, 1805

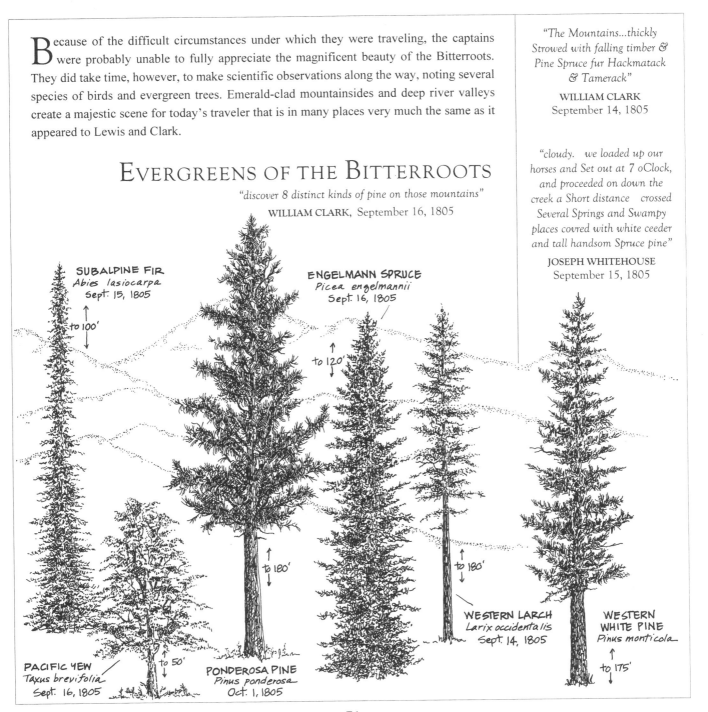

SUBALPINE FIR
Abies lasiocarpa
Sept. 15, 1805
to 100'

ENGELMANN SPRUCE
Picea engelmannii
Sept. 16, 1805
to 120'

to 180'

WESTERN LARCH
Larix occidentalis
Sept. 14, 1805
to 180'

WESTERN WHITE PINE
Pinus monticola
to 175'

PACIFIC YEW
Taxus brevifolia
Sept. 16, 1805
to 50'

PONDEROSA PINE
Pinus ponderosa
Oct. 1, 1805

"The want of provisions together with the dificul[t]y of passing those emence mountains dampened the sperits of the party."

WILLIAM CLARK
September 18, 1805

"I find myself growing weak for the want of food and most of the men complain of a similar deficiency, and have fallen off very much."

MERIWETHER LEWIS
September 21, 1805

The Want of Food

"and with meager provisions..."

By the time the Corps of Discovery reached the Bitterroots, their supply of food staples was very nearly depleted. Because game was scarce, they had to make do with what little they could find and stretch what little they had left. They were compelled to kill colts for meat. With some crayfish, a few grouse, a coyote, and what was left of their "horse beef," they made "one more hearty meal, not knowing where the next was to be found."

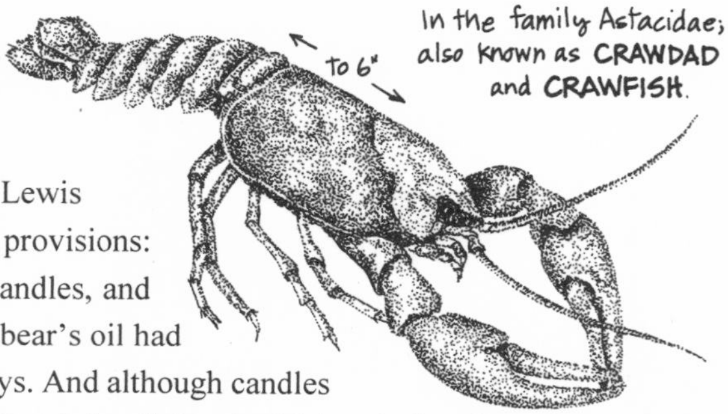

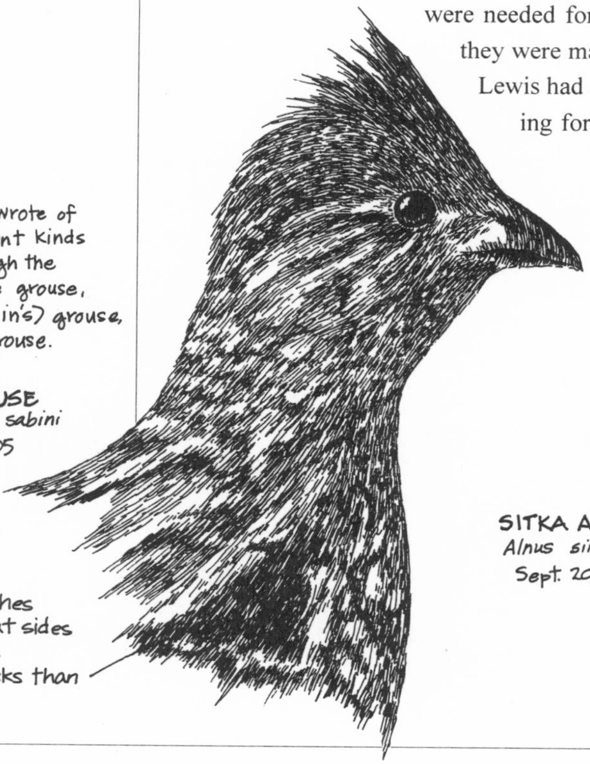

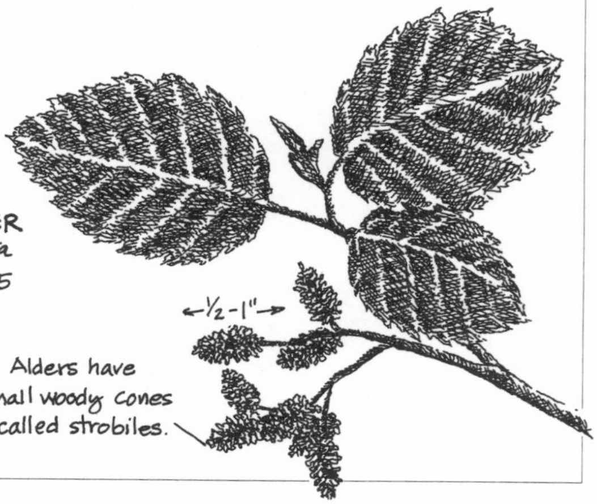

CRAYFISH
In the family Astacidae; also known as CRAWDAD and CRAWFISH.
To 6"

At one desperate point, Captain Lewis listed what remained in their stock of provisions: a little bear's oil, twenty pounds of candles, and a few canisters of portable soup. The bear's oil had been saved from earlier, game-rich days. And although candles were needed for giving light, the high-calorie tallow from which they were made could be used as an emergency ration. Captain Lewis had ordered 193 pounds of portable soup while preparing for the expedition. He had correctly reasoned that at some point they would experience a critical food shortage and had purchased the concentrated soup to guard against starvation. Although some of the men disliked the soup, it helped sustain them through the Bitterroot Mountains.

Captain Lewis wrote of seeing 3 different kinds of grouse through the Bitterroots: blue grouse, spruce (or Franklin's) grouse, and ruffed grouse.
RUFFED GROUSE
Bonasa umbellus sabini
Sept. 20, 1805
Dark-colored patches of ruff feathers at sides of neck are more prominent on cocks than hens.

SITKA ALDER
Alnus sinuata
Sept. 20, 1805
←½-1"→
Alders have small woody cones called strobiles.

Portable soup was probably a beef, mutton, or veal broth, condensed by long hours of boiling and stored in the form of dried cakes or a thick liquid; it may also have included powdered grains and vegetables. To prevent spoiling, it was kept in glass or tin containers. This type of emergency food had apparently been used by the military for some time—particularly to feed the sick. Captain Lewis felt strongly that portable soup was an essential item for the expedition; the price he paid, $289.50, was more than he spent on any other type of provisions.

> *"without a miracle it was impossible to feed 30 hungry men...*
> *So Capt. Lewis gave out some portable soup, which he had along,*
> *to be used in cases of necessity."*
>
> PATRICK GASS, September 14, 1805

Following is a very simplified version of portable soup based on a recipe used in the late eighteenth century and found in Dr. Eldon Chuinard's book *Only One Man Died.* This soup represents the reconstituted product that corps members ate on cold, hungry evenings in the Bitterroot Mountains.

PORTABLE SOUP

In a small saucepan combine using wire whip:
- 2 cups fat-free beef broth
- 5 teaspoons barley flour
- 5 teaspoons bean flour

Stir together over medium heat until thick and bubbly. Reduce heat and simmer, stirring, for 5 more minutes. Serve hot with salt and pepper. Makes about 2 cups— enough to give several people a sample.

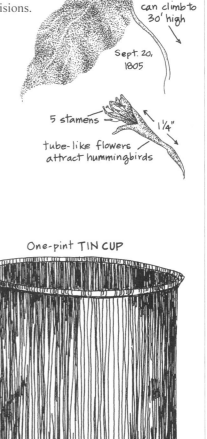

ORANGE HONEYSUCKLE
Lonicera ciliosa

can climb to 30' high

Sept. 20, 1805

5 stamens — 1¼"

tube-like flowers attract hummingbirds

One-pint TIN CUP

18th century design
PEWTER SPOON

HORN SPOON carved in the fiddleback shape

(Illinois State Museum, Springfield, IL)

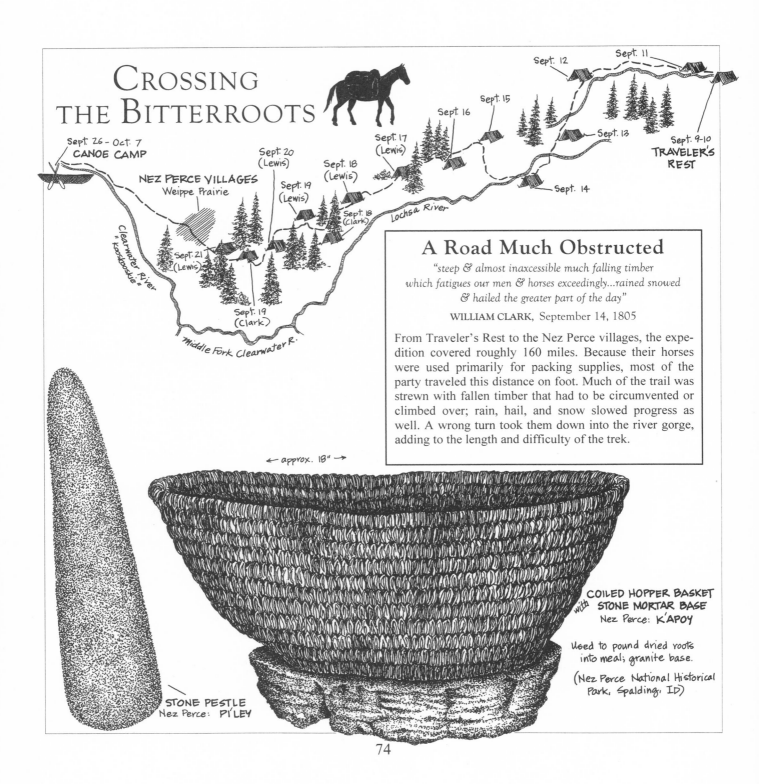

CROSSING THE BITTERROOTS

Sept. 26 - Oct. 7
CANOE CAMP

NEZ PERCE VILLAGES
Weippe Prairie

Sept. 20 (Lewis)

Sept. 19 (Lewis)

Sept. 18 (Lewis)

Sept. 17 (Lewis)

Sept. 18 (Clark)

Sept. 21 (Lewis)

Sept. 19 (Clark)

Clearwater River "Kooskooskie"

Middle Fork Clearwater R.

Lochsa River

Sept. 16

Sept. 15

Sept. 12

Sept. 11

Sept. 13

Sept. 14

Sept. 9-10
TRAVELER'S REST

A Road Much Obstructed

"steep & almost inaxcessible much falling timber which fatigues our men & horses exceedingly...rained snowed & hailed the greater part of the day"

WILLIAM CLARK, September 14, 1805

From Traveler's Rest to the Nez Perce villages, the expedition covered roughly 160 miles. Because their horses were used primarily for packing supplies, most of the party traveled this distance on foot. Much of the trail was strewn with fallen timber that had to be circumvented or climbed over; rain, hail, and snow slowed progress as well. A wrong turn took them down into the river gorge, adding to the length and difficulty of the trek.

← approx. 18" →

COILED HOPPER BASKET
with STONE MORTAR BASE
Nez Perce: **K'APOY**

Used to pound dried roots into meal; granite base.

(Nez Perce National Historical Park, Spalding, ID)

STONE PESTLE
Nez Perce: **PI'LEY**

Descending Once More
"what a triumph in camp that night"

After several days of struggling to conquer the Bitterroots, Captain Clark and six hunters pressed on ahead in search of game for the nearly starving travelers. On their first day out they were rewarded with a reassuring view: a large plain in the distant southwest that promised not only the potential for something to eat, but also an end to the seemingly infinite mountain range. On September 20, 1805, Clark and his group met the Nez Perce, who welcomed them with a meal of dried salmon, roots, berries, and buffalo meat. Two days later Lewis and the remaining corps members joined Clark at the Nez Perce village. Exhaustion could not dampen their triumph in emerging victorious from "those rugged, winding mountains."

CAMAS
Camassia quamash

1-2'

BISCUITROOT
Nez Perce: **LAQÁPTAT**

Dug during June and July, this root was second in importance only to camas. It was eaten raw, cooked, or dried and was ground to make porridge & finger cakes.

BITTERROOT
Nez Perce: **KÍTA·N**

Bitterroot was boiled to remove the bitter taste and was served plain or seasoned with berries and fat.

CAMAS
Nez Perce: **QÉMES**

A digging stick (see page 61) was used to pry up these deep-growing bulbs. Camas was baked and eaten fresh or dried and ground to make porridge & bread.

"there was as much joy and rejoicing among the corps, as happens among passengers at sea, who have experienced a dangerous and protracted voyage, when they first discover land on the long looked for coast."
PATRICK GASS
September 19, 1805

"the pleasure I now felt in having tryumphed over the rockey Mountains and decending once more to a level and fertile country where there was every rational hope of finding a comfortable subsistence for myself and party can be more readily conceived than expressed, nor was the flattering prospect of the final success of the expedition less pleasing."
MERIWETHER LEWIS
September 22, 1805

Weippe Prairie

Captain Clark's party encountered the Nez Perce in a beautiful mountain prairie known for its abundant supply of camas. The root of this plant (a member of the lily family) formed a principal part of the Nez Perce diet. In the spring of 1806, Captain Lewis described the stunning beauty of camas blooming on the prairie:

"the quawmash is now in blume and from the colour of its bloom at a short distance it resembles lakes of fine clear water, so complete is this deseption that on first sight I could have swoarn it was water."

ADZE

Used to smooth and shape logs, the adze was especially valuable for making dugout canoes.

About Building Canoes

"Set all the men able to work ab!. building canoes"

WILLIAM CLARK
September 27, 1805

After felling, the log was squared and the ends trimmed. The top was notched and cut away, then burned to create a hollow. When the hollow was sufficiently deepened, water was sprinkled on it to stop the burning process. Using this method they made five canoes in ten days.

The Nez Perce treated the Corps of Discovery with generous hospitality, providing food for the famished group as well as a description of the country to the west. Unfortunately, the Nez Perce staples of dried salmon and camas root didn't agree with the men—most likely because it was radically different from the predominantly meat diet to which they were accustomed. As a consequence, most of the party became violently ill and remained so for several days. Those who were strong enough built canoes from ponderosa pine logs, using the Nez Perce method of burning out a hollow. This technique proved easier for the ailing men.

On October 7, with two Nez Perce chiefs along to promote diplomacy, the Lewis and Clark Expedition put their canoes into the Clearwater River and began the last leg of their journey to the "Great Western Ocean."

CANOE CAMP

Site where canoes were built to finish the journey.

Orofino, ID

THE LIST

mule deer antler

white-tailed deer antler

What a thrill it must have been for Lewis and Clark to make scientific discoveries as they explored their way across the continent. Animal discoveries played a fascinating—and sometimes fearsome—part.

It's not hard to imagine the merriment around evening campfires where anecdotes were surely told of creatures they had met with during the day. Tales of prairie dogs that stubbornly evaded capture or of grizzly bears that chased hunters up trees and into rivers. Recollections of amazingly close calls with rattlesnakes and buffalo. Accounts of game in every direction "as far as the eye of the observer could reach." These firsthand experiences, faithfully recounted in the journals, give us a glimpse into the grand beauty and persistent challenges of the animal world they encountered.

The List

As the corps went west
They listed creatures (some were new
to science)—let me tell you, there were really quite a few.
Here is just a sample of what they encountered there;
Try and sing them if you think you dare!

Sockeye salmon, Clark's nutcracker, pronghorn antelope,
Ring-necked duck, jack rabbit,
Western willet, mountain goat;
Beaver, black-billed magpie, and the one with the most scare:
Ursus horribilis, also known as grizzly bear.

Candlefish, elk, warty salamander, pelican,
Lewis's woodpecker, porcupine,
And whistling swan;
Rattlesnake, tern, sturgeon, and the biggest of the eaters:
Those unremitting, troublesome, and pesky ol' "musqutors."

Steller's jay, kit fox, coyote,
Columbian sharp-tailed grouse,
Prairie dog and weasel, cutthroat trout, white-fronted goose;
Whooping crane, seal, badger, and the one that they loved so:
The tongue especially—and the hump—that tasty buffalo.

Yellow-bellied marmot,
Ermine, bighorn sheep, condor,
Gray wolf, bull snake, western pileated woodpecker;
Oregon bobcat, snow goose, mule deer, trumpeter swan—
I'm out of breath, so now this song is done!

BLACK-TAILED PRAIRIE DOG
Cynomys ludovicianus
Sept. 7, 1804

"the Village of those animals Cov.ᵈ about 4 acres...and Contains great numbers of holes on the top of which those little animals Set erect make a Whistleing noise and whin allarmed Step into their hole. we por'd into one of the holes 5 barrels of Water without filling it."

WILLIAM CLARK, September 7, 1804

In order to provide accurate journal descriptions, the captains examined animal specimens carefully—often in minute detail. They noted color, size, and shape; they measured, counted, and dissected. Habitats were observed, as were calls and songs, eating habits, range, and distribution. This information was then carefully recorded, providing future zoologists with the necessary data for correct classification.

LEWIS'S WOODPECKER
Asyndesmus lewis

July 20, 1805

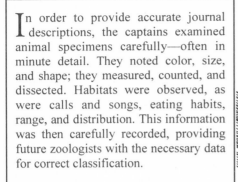

"The Black woodpecker...is found in most parts of the roky Mountains as well as the Western and S.W. mountains... this bird is about the size of the lark woodpecker or the turtle dove, tho' it's wings are longer than either of those birds.   the beak is black, one inch long...and sharply pointed...the belly and breast is a curious mixture of white and blood reed which has much the appearance of having been artificially painted"

MERIWETHER LEWIS, May 27, 1806

"The legs of this bear are somewhat longer than those of the black, as are it's tallons and tusks...it's colour is yellowish brown, the eyes small, black, and piercing; the front of the fore legs near the feet is usually black; the fur is finer thicker and deeper than that of the black bear...it is a much more furious and formidable anamal, and will frequently pursue the hunter when wounded.   it is asstonishing to see the wounds they will bear before they can be put to death."

MERIWETHER LEWIS
April 29, 1805

GRIZZLY BEAR
Ursus arctos horribilis
Apr. 29, 1805

"in my walk I Killed a Buck Goat of this Countery, about the hight of the Grown Deer...the Colour is a light gray with black behind its ears down its neck, and its face white round its neck, its Sides and its rump round its tail which is Short & white: Verry actively made, has only a pair of hoofs to each foot, his brains on the back of his head, his Norstrals large, his eyes like a Sheep he is more like the Antilope or Gazella of Africa than any other Species of Goat."

WILLIAM CLARK, September 14, 1804

"Colter Killed...a curious kind of Deer (Mule Deer) of a Dark gray Col: more so than common, hair long & fine, the ears large & long...the Taile about the length of Common Deer, round (like a Cow) a tuft of black hair about the end, this Spec[i]es of Deer jumps like a goat or Sheep"

WILLIAM CLARK, September 17, 1804

PRONGHORN
Antilocapra americana
Sept. 14, 1804

MULE DEER
Odocoileus hemionus
Sept. 17, 1804

"Killed a serpent on the bank of the river adjoining a large prarie.

Length from nose to tail   5 F   2. Inch
Circumpherence in largest part   4 $^1/_2$
Number of scuta on belly   221.
D^o. on Tale   53

No pison teeth...two roes of black spots on a lite yellow ground pass throughout his whole length on the upper points of the scuta of the belly and tale $^1/_2$ Inch apart this snake is vulgarly called the cow or bull snake from a bellowing nois which it is said sometimes to make resembling that anamal, tho' as to this fact I am unable to attest it never having heard them make that or any other nois myself."

MERIWETHER LEWIS, August 5, 1804

BULL SNAKE
Pituophis sayi sayi
Aug. 5, 1804

After tasting their first buffalo (killed by Joseph Field on August 23, 1804), tongue and hump became a favored delicacy among the men. They relied on the meat of these large, lumbering beasts to keep the party fed as they traveled through the Plains. When they had more fresh meat than needed, they turned the excess into jerky by drying it in the sun or smoking it over small fires or both. The jerky, or "jurk" as the hunters called it, was then stored away for future, leaner times.

"in the evening Drewyer and Frazier arrived with about 800 lb. of excellent dryed meat and about 100 lb. of tallow."

MERIWETHER LEWIS, June 25, 1805

Some grocery store meat departments carry domestically grown buffalo from time to time. If you are fortunate enough to locate this lean, low cholesterol meat, you can try your hand at making buffalo jerky. The following recipe is for a tasty precooked jerky, as recommended by the Washington State University Cooperative Extension.*

BUFFALO JERKY

SELECTION OF MEAT:
The best jerky is made from lean meat. The leaner the meat, the better the finished product. Either fresh or frozen meat can be used. Good cuts for jerky are the flank, round, sirloin, or rump cuts.

MEAT PREPARATION:
Meat used for jerky should be sliced into long $^3/_{16}$ to $^1/_4$-inch-thick slices. For a tender jerky, cut the meat across the grain. For a tougher, more chewy product, cut the meat with the grain. Remove all the fat possible. For easier cutting, partially freeze the meat. Use a sharp knife or electric meat slicer.

BUFFALO (BISON)
Bison bison

"when I arrived in sight of the white-bear Islands the missouri bottoms on both sides of the river were crouded with buffaloe   I sincerely beleif that there were not less than 10 thousand buffaloe within a circle of 2 miles arround that place."

MERIWETHER LEWIS, July 11, 1806

BISON HORN SPOON
Nez Perce: QOQA·LX SÓ·X

(Nez Perce National Historical Park, Spalding, ID)

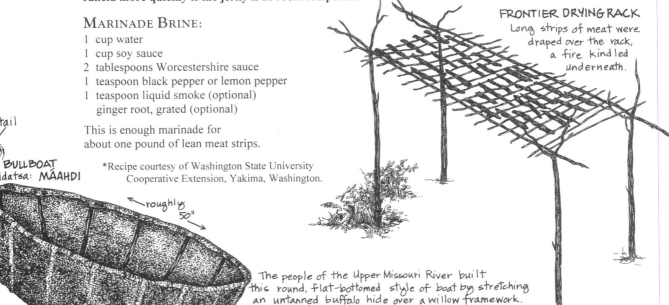

BISON SCAPULA HOE
Hidatsa: AWA-ÉHE

PRECOOK JERKY PIECES:

1. Prepare 1 to 2 cups of marinade brine (see below) and put in large saucepan.
2. Bring the marinade to a full rolling boil over medium heat. Add a few meat strips, making sure that they are covered by marinade. Reheat to a full boil.
3. Remove the pan from the range. Using tongs, immediately remove meat from the hot marinade to prevent overcooking.
4. Repeat steps 2 and 3 until all meat has been precooked. Add more marinade if necessary.

Caution: Soaking the meat strips in marinade overnight is not advised. Putting unmarinated strips directly into boiling marinade minimizes a cooked flavor and maintains safety.

DRYING THE MEAT:

Either a dehydrator or smoker can be used to dry the precooked meat pieces. Put the precooked meat in a single layer on drying racks. The strips should not overlap since air circulation is very important.

Test for doneness by letting a piece cool. When cool, it should crack but not break when bent. **There should not be any moist or underdone spots.**

Refrigerate the jerky overnight in a plastic freezer bag. Then check again for proper dryness. If necessary, dry longer.

Store jerky in plastic freezer bags or glass jars. For long-term storage, put the jerky in a refrigerator or freezer. Jerky can be stored at room temperature for short periods of time, but **the fat will turn rancid more quickly if the jerky is at room temperature.**

MARINADE BRINE:

1 cup water
1 cup soy sauce
2 tablespoons Worcestershire sauce
1 teaspoon black pepper or lemon pepper
1 teaspoon liquid smoke (optional)
   ginger root, grated (optional)

This is enough marinade for
about one pound of lean meat strips.

*Recipe courtesy of Washington State University
Cooperative Extension, Yakima, Washington.

FRONTIER DRYING RACK
Long strips of meat were
draped over the rack,
a fire kindled
underneath.

tail

BULLBOAT
Hidatsa: MÁAHDI

←roughly
50"→

The people of the Upper Missouri River built
this round, flat-bottomed style of boat by stretching
an untanned buffalo hide over a willow framework.

81

Lewis and Clark are credited with discovering 12 new species or subspecies of fish, 15 of reptiles and amphibians, and 44 of mammals. The largest category of their new-to-science animal encounters was birds, with 51 new species or subspecies recorded. They observed birds throughout the entire course of the journey—migrating birds and resident birds, birds of the mountain, the prairie, the shore.

"Great numbers of Birds are seen in those Plains, Such as black bird, ren, [wren] or Prarie burd, a kind of larke about the sise of a Partridge with a Short tail, &c."
WILLIAM CLARK, August 25, 1804

Learning to identify birds—by both sight *and* sound—is an inexpensive, satisfying hobby for all ages. Bird watching is fun to do alone or with a companion; it's a pleasing, lifelong activity that can be enjoyed in any part of the world.

BIRD WATCHING

Supplies:

♦ binoculars
♦ bird identification guide(s)
♦ notebook & pencil

With identification guide and binoculars in hand, begin to observe and identify the birds in your own neighborhood. Listen for calls, notice habitats. Learn which birds are residents in your area and which migrate through (and when their migration usually occurs). If possible, place a feeder where you can easily watch from a window. (Black-oil sunflower seeds are a favorite of many birds. Niger thistle is another important birdseed, especially if you want to attract goldfinches; because it is a tiny seed, you will want to use a feeder designed specifically for thistle.) A hummingbird feeder and birdbath will attract even more birds to your backyard.

In your notebook, keep a list of the new birds you see. Jot down identifying characteristics, e.g., color, size, markings, beak shape. Note flight patterns and feeding habits. Be sure to record the date, especially if it is a migratory bird, so that you will know when to look for that species the following year.

After you have learned to identify birds by sight, start to develop song and call recognition. Several excellent audio recordings are available for this purpose. Some people find that associating an English word or phrase with the call helps them remember the call better. The black-capped chickadee is easy to recognize because it sings its own name: "Chick-a-dee-dee-dee." The California quail is known for its loud "Chi-ca´-go," and the American robin for calling "Cheer-up!" Remember to write the calls in your notebook for future identification.

steller's jay

MONTANA HORNED OWL
Bubo virginianus occidentalis

Apr. 14, 1806

black-billed magpie

1½"

"the egg is of a bluish brown colour, freckled with redish brown spots."
MERIWETHER LEWIS
April 14, 1805

"bright indigo blue... with small transverse stripes of black"
MERIWETHER LEWIS
May 26, 1805

broad-tailed hummingbird

egg & nest actual size

"found the nest of a humming bird, it had just began to lay its eggs."
MERIWETHER LEWIS, June 15, 1806

WE PROCEEDED ON

"We proceeded on..."

Used repeatedly throughout the journals, this simple phrase reflects the determined commitment of expedition members to push on, to endure, to do all that was in their strength to continue. The trials they faced were varied—from the small, but incredibly irritating (those pesky mosquitoes), to the nearly insurmountable and life threatening.

Four major geographic challenges defied their progression: ascending the Missouri River, portaging around the Great Falls of the Missouri, crossing over the Rocky Mountains, and navigating the rapids and falls of the Columbia River. Meeting these barriers with vigor, ingenuity, and endurance, the Corps of Discovery steadfastly proceeded on.

Large blue-black berries; a favorite of berry pickers in the Pacific Northwest.

Described Feb. 7, 1806

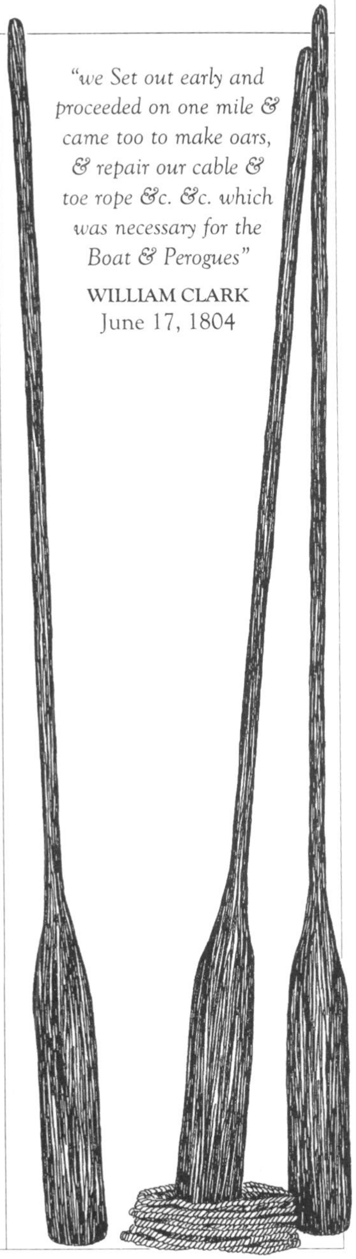

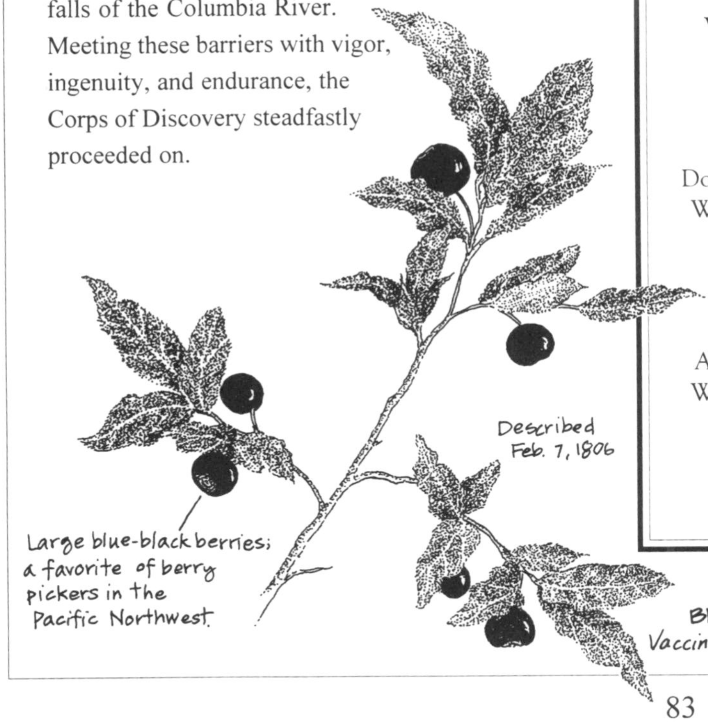

BLACK HUCKLEBERRY
Vaccinium membranaceum

We Proceeded On

We proceeded on,
We proceeded on—
Up the Missouri's flow
We our oars did row,
We proceeded on.

We proceeded on,
We proceeded on—
Great Falls we skirted wide
To reach the other side,
We proceeded on.

We proceeded on,
We proceeded on—
O'er the Rockies tall
We endured our call,
We proceeded on.

We proceeded on,
We proceeded on—
Down the Columbia deep
We the rapids did meet,
We proceeded on.

We proceeded on,
We proceeded on—
All the journey through
We were brave and true,
We proceeded on.

We proceeded on.

"we Set out early and proceeded on one mile & came too to make oars, & repair our cable & toe rope &c. &c. which was necessary for the Boat & Perogues"
WILLIAM CLARK
June 17, 1804

PINK CLEOME
Cleome serrulata
Aug. 25, 1804

"growth of the open prairie"

to 3'

Also known as
ROCKY MT.
BEE PLANT

"Up the Missouri's flow..."

Also known as the "Mighty Mo," the Missouri River is the largest tributary of the Mississippi. It flows over 2,300 miles from its source in the Rocky Mountains to its mouth on the Mississippi, passing through or forming the border of seven states: Montana, North Dakota, South Dakota, Nebraska, Iowa, Kansas, and Missouri. Because of a high sediment content, pioneers dubbed it the "Big Muddy."

Although the Missouri River did have hazards (banks that would suddenly give way, hidden snags, and sand bars), the most wearing difficulty for the Lewis and Clark Expedition was battling against the river's current, day in and day out. With experienced rivermen keeping watch at the bow, crew members at times resorted to pushing with setting poles or hauling on towlines to coax the boats upstream. Progressing up the Missouri was a time-consuming, backbreaking process.

BIGHORN
Ovis canadensis
auduboni
Apr. 26, 1805

Horns may grow to
more than 4 feet.

WHITE CLIFFS of the MISSOURI

"Seven Sisters"

"The hills and river Clifts which we passed today exhibit a most romantic appearance....they are formed of remarkable white sandstone which is sufficiently soft to give way readily to the impression of water...which with the help of a little immagination and an oblique view, at a distance are made to represent eligant ranges of lofty freestone buildings"

MERIWETHER LEWIS, May 31, 1805

THE MISSOURI RIVER

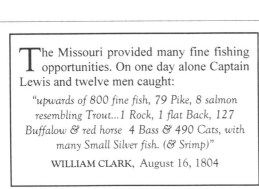

The Missouri provided many fine fishing opportunities. On one day alone Captain Lewis and twelve men caught:

"upwards of 800 fine fish, 79 Pike, 8 salmon resembling Trout...1 Rock, 1 flat Back, 127 Buffalow & red horse 4 Bass & 490 Cats, with many Small Silver fish. (& Srimp)"

WILLIAM CLARK, August 16, 1804

WHOOPING CRANE
Grus americana

WHITE PELICAN
Pelecanus erythrorhynchos

BLUE CATFISH
Ictalurus furcatus
Aug. 25, 1804

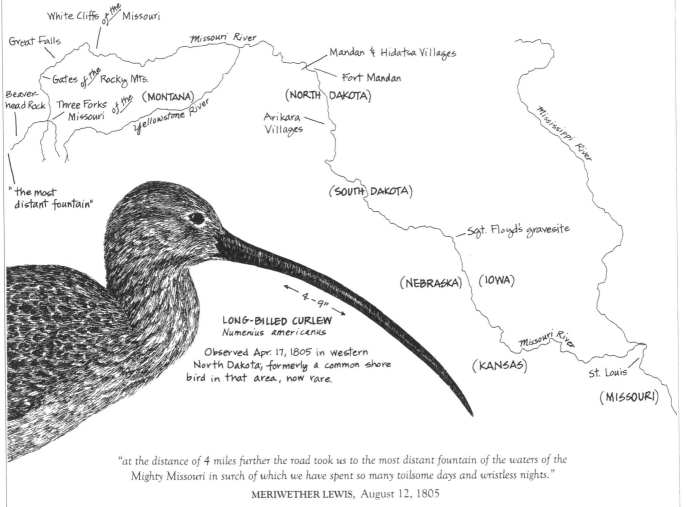

White Cliffs of the Missouri

Great Falls

Gates of the Rocky Mts.

Beaver-head Rock

Three Forks of the Missouri

(MONTANA)

Missouri River

Yellowstone River

"the most distant fountain"

Mandan & Hidatsa Villages

Fort Mandan

(NORTH DAKOTA)

Arikara Villages

(SOUTH DAKOTA)

Mississippi River

Sgt. Floyd's gravesite

(NEBRASKA)

(IOWA)

Missouri River

(KANSAS)

St. Louis

(MISSOURI)

4 - 9"

LONG-BILLED CURLEW
Numenius americanus

Observed Apr. 17, 1805 in western North Dakota; formerly a common shore bird in that area, now rare.

"at the distance of 4 miles further the road took us to the most distant fountain of the waters of the Mighty Missouri in surch of which we have spent so many toilsome days and wristless nights."

MERIWETHER LEWIS, August 12, 1805

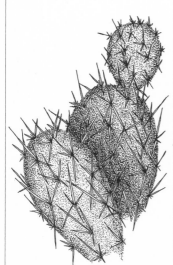

PLAINS PRICKLY PEAR
Opuntia polyacantha

"Great Falls we skirted wide..."

Relying on information provided by the Hidatsas, Captain Lewis was expecting to find a large waterfall when he and a few men went scouting on June 11, 1805. He wasn't disappointed. Two days later he first heard, then witnessed, what he described as a "truly magnificent and sublimely grand object." The Missouri River cascaded over an eighty-seven-foot ledge, creating a spectacular scene that both astonished Lewis and filled him with pleasure.

His astonishment was multiplied the next day when further upstream he discovered four additional waterfalls. While this impressive set of falls was a thrill to behold, it presented a predicament to the Corps of Discovery. They had anticipated only one—not five—falls. Hauling their cargo overland around the falls would be much more difficult than they had envisioned.

On June 22, 1805, the portage began. Carriages with wheels cut from a cottonwood tree transformed two of the canoes into wagons for carrying baggage. Unnecessary articles and reserve food for the trip home were cached away. Even so, the approximately eighteen-mile portage required several wearisome, and often painful, trips.

Missouri River

"Great Falls"
(87 ft., ¾ in.)

"Crooked Falls"
(19 ft.)

Colter Falls
(6 ft., 7 in.;
descent 14 ft., 7 in.)

Rainbow Falls
"Beautiful Cascade"
(47 ft., 8 in.)

Black Eagle Falls
"Upper Pitch"
(26 ft., 5 in.)

PORTAGE ROUTE

Breakdowns caused frustrating delays. Prickly pear cactus punctured feet. Strength was stretched to the point of exhaustion. On July 2, after eleven grueling days, the portage was complete.

THE GREAT FALLS PORTAGE

"I direct stakes to be cut to stick up in the prarie to show the way for the party to transport the baggage...soon after we set out it began to rain and continued a short time we proceeded on thro' a tolerable leavel plain"

WILLIAM CLARK, June 20, 1805

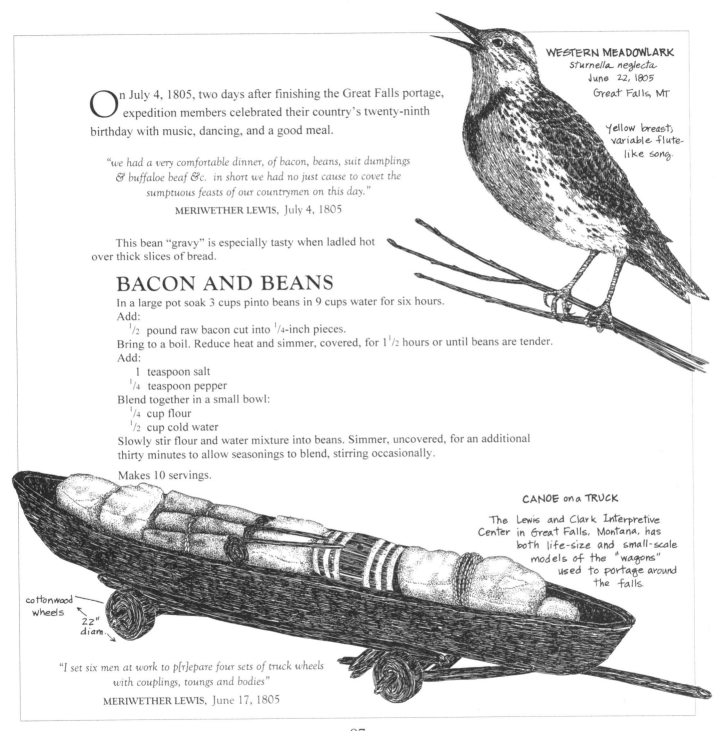

On July 4, 1805, two days after finishing the Great Falls portage, expedition members celebrated their country's twenty-ninth birthday with music, dancing, and a good meal.

"we had a very comfortable dinner, of bacon, beans, suit dumplings & buffaloe beaf &c. in short we had no just cause to covet the sumptuous feasts of our countrymen on this day."

MERIWETHER LEWIS, July 4, 1805

This bean "gravy" is especially tasty when ladled hot over thick slices of bread.

BACON AND BEANS

In a large pot soak 3 cups pinto beans in 9 cups water for six hours.
Add:
  $1/2$ pound raw bacon cut into $1/4$-inch pieces.
Bring to a boil. Reduce heat and simmer, covered, for $1 1/2$ hours or until beans are tender.
Add:
   1 teaspoon salt
  $1/4$ teaspoon pepper
Blend together in a small bowl:
  $1/4$ cup flour
  $1/2$ cup cold water
Slowly stir flour and water mixture into beans. Simmer, uncovered, for an additional thirty minutes to allow seasonings to blend, stirring occasionally.

Makes 10 servings.

WESTERN MEADOWLARK
Sturnella neglecta
June 22, 1805
Great Falls, MT

Yellow breast; variable flute-like song.

CANOE on a TRUCK

The Lewis and Clark Interpretive Center in Great Falls, Montana, has both life-size and small-scale models of the "wagons" used to portage around the falls.

cottonwood wheels
22" diam.

"I set six men at work to p[r]epare four sets of truck wheels with couplings, toungs and bodies"

MERIWETHER LEWIS, June 17, 1805

MOUNTAIN GOAT
Oreamnos americanus
Aug. 24, 1805

"O'er the Rockies tall..."

Described by Captain Lewis as "lofty," "immense," and "formidable," this massive range extends more than 3,000 miles through the United States and Canada, forming the Continental Divide. It offers breathtaking scenery to the traveler: snow-capped peaks, glacial lakes, and sparkling mountain streams. For the Corps of Discovery, traveling by boat, by horse, and on foot, the Rockies became a daunting foe to be conquered. Lack of game and harsh weather complicated the task of crossing over rough territory. Their success can be largely credited to the capable assistance of the Shoshoni and Nez Perce guides who escorted them through much of this region.

"this morning we set out early and proceeded on very well tho' the water appears to encrease in volocity as we advance....this evening we entered much the most remarkable clifts that we have yet seen. these clifts rise from the waters edge on either side perpendicularly to the hight of (about) 1200 feet. every object here wears a dark and gloomy aspect. the tow[er]ing and projecting rocks in many places seem ready to tumble on us. the river appears to have forced it's way through this immence body of solid rock for the distance of 5 ³/₄ Miles and where it makes it's exit below has th[r]own on either side vast collumns of rocks mountains high....I called it the gates of the rocky mounatains."

MERIWETHER LEWIS
July 19, 1805

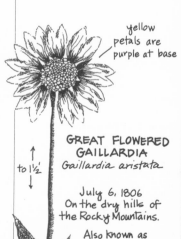

yellow petals are purple at base

GREAT FLOWERED GAILLARDIA
Gaillardia aristata

to 1½'

July 6, 1806
On the dry hills of the Rocky Mountains.

Also known as
INDIAN BLANKET and **BLANKETFLOWER**

GATES of the MOUNTAINS
near Helena, MT

As the expedition entered the Rocky Mountains, of foremost concern was locating the Shoshoni Indians from whom they hoped to purchase horses. (A lengthy portage from the headwaters of the Missouri to the headwaters of rivers flowing west would require horses for transporting necessary baggage.) They passed through (or skirted) several small ranges in this quest, including the Big Belt, Tobacco Root, and Beaverhead Mountains. The river became increasingly difficult to navigate—at some places shallow and rocky, at others rapid and rough. Fatigued from days of pulling heavily laden dugout canoes, the men's spirits flagged.

Approaching Sacagawea's homeland, they began to see encouraging signs of her people: smoke in the distance, tracks, and recently inhabited willow-brush lodges. Sacagawea recognized landmarks and assured the captains that they were on the correct route. After weeks of searching, Captain Lewis and a small scouting party finally made contact with three Shoshoni women who led the men to their village. The expedition soon made camp (known as Camp Fortunate), and the negotiation for horses began.

One of the most amazing chapters of the entire expedition occurred as talks with the Shoshoni were just commencing. Sacagawea suddenly realized that the Chief—Cameahwait—was her brother. Normally quiet and calm, Sacagawea wept uncontrollably. This remarkable, touching reunion was undoubtedly an important factor in Lewis and Clark's successful negotiation for horses. Without those horses, the expedition wouldn't have made it over the Rocky Mountains.

↑ 5-11"

↑ 3-6"

"we proceeded on to the top of the dividing ridge from which I discovered immence ranges of high mountains still to the West of us with their tops partially covered with snow."
MERIWETHER LEWIS
August 12, 1805

PONDEROSA PINE
Pinus ponderosa
The Shoshoni peeled bark from pine trees to obtain sap and the soft interior parts for food.

"proceeded on over verry high mountains which was verry bad for our horses to climb up and down them....we descended a Mountain nearly as Steep as the roof of a house."
JOSEPH WHITEHOUSE
September 1, 1805

"at the distance of about 4 miles we passed 4 small rivulets near each other on which we saw som resent bowers or small conic lodges formed with willow brush."
MERIWETHER LEWIS
August 12, 1805

WILLOW-BRUSH LODGE
A cone-shaped frame covered with brush & grasses.

Also called
WICKIUP

"Down the Columbia deep..."

From its Canadian Rocky Mountain source, the Columbia River flows generally south through Washington State to the Oregon border, then stretches west to the Pacific Ocean. Extending 1,214 miles, this salmon-rich river is now checked by several dams which provide electricity and irrigation water to the region. Because of the dams, we can no longer see the spectacular rapids and falls with which the expedition contended.

The first major Columbia River barrier to be overcome by the explorers was Celilo Falls, a principal fishing area. With the assistance of local Indians, they portaged around the most difficult portion of this cataract, which Captain Clark called "the great falls."

The next two barriers came at The Dalles. This set began with an "agitated gut swelling" stretch called the Short Narrows, then continued a few miles farther on with the Long Narrows. The captains chose to have nonswimmers carry their most valuable articles around both of these treacherous areas while those who could swim took the canoes (which were too large to portage) through the turbulence. Indians lined the banks to watch the daring canoeists; they were astonished to see corps members come through safely.

The last of the major obstacles, the "Great Shute," came just east of Beacon Rock. After portaging their baggage around this tempestuous, rocky stretch, they coaxed the canoes over the rocks on poles placed from one boulder to another.

The Columbia River ride was fraught with danger; that they made it without loss of life is a wonder.

↑
850'
↓

BEACON ROCK
Washington

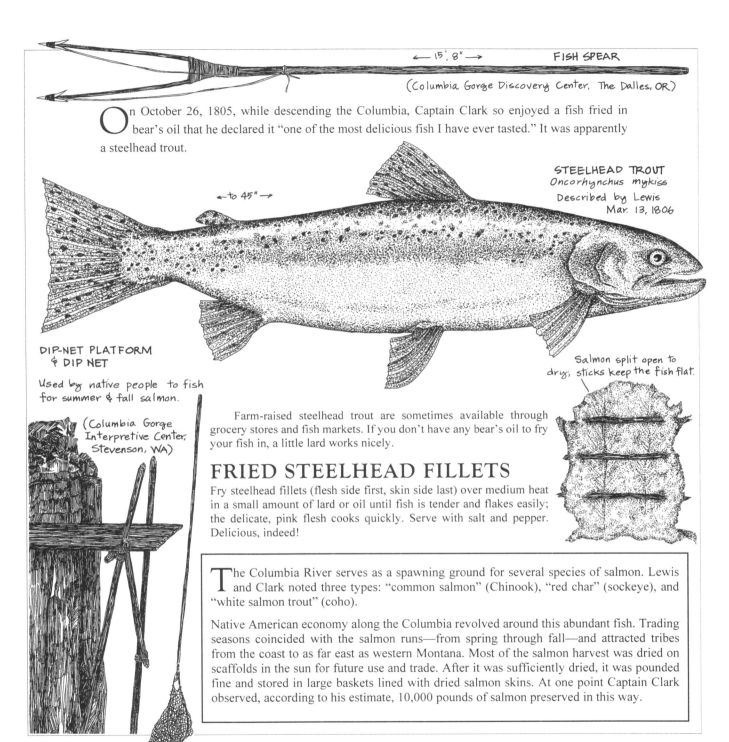

← 15' 8" → FISH SPEAR

(Columbia Gorge Discovery Center, The Dalles, OR)

On October 26, 1805, while descending the Columbia, Captain Clark so enjoyed a fish fried in bear's oil that he declared it "one of the most delicious fish I have ever tasted." It was apparently a steelhead trout.

STEELHEAD TROUT
Oncorhynchus mykiss
Described by Lewis
Mar. 13, 1806

← to 45" →

DIP-NET PLATFORM & DIP NET

Used by native people to fish for summer & fall salmon.

(Columbia Gorge Interpretive Center, Stevenson, WA)

Salmon split open to dry; sticks keep the fish flat.

Farm-raised steelhead trout are sometimes available through grocery stores and fish markets. If you don't have any bear's oil to fry your fish in, a little lard works nicely.

FRIED STEELHEAD FILLETS

Fry steelhead fillets (flesh side first, skin side last) over medium heat in a small amount of lard or oil until fish is tender and flakes easily; the delicate, pink flesh cooks quickly. Serve with salt and pepper. Delicious, indeed!

The Columbia River serves as a spawning ground for several species of salmon. Lewis and Clark noted three types: "common salmon" (Chinook), "red char" (sockeye), and "white salmon trout" (coho).

Native American economy along the Columbia revolved around this abundant fish. Trading seasons coincided with the salmon runs—from spring through fall—and attracted tribes from the coast to as far east as western Montana. Most of the salmon harvest was dried on scaffolds in the sun for future use and trade. After it was sufficiently dried, it was pounded fine and stored in large baskets lined with dried salmon skins. At one point Captain Clark observed, according to his estimate, 10,000 pounds of salmon preserved in this way.

91

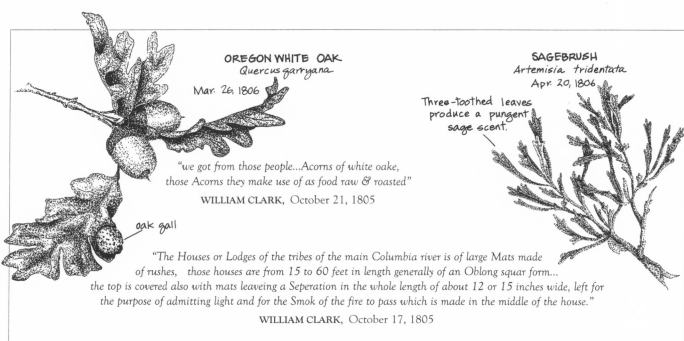

OREGON WHITE OAK
Quercus garryana
Mar. 26, 1806

oak gall

*"we got from those people...Acorns of white oake,
those Acorns they make use of as food raw & roasted"*

WILLIAM CLARK, October 21, 1805

SAGEBRUSH
Artemisia tridentata
Apr. 20, 1806

Three-toothed leaves
produce a pungent
sage scent.

*"The Houses or Lodges of the tribes of the main Columbia river is of large Mats made
of rushes, those houses are from 15 to 60 feet in length generally of an Oblong squar form...
the top is covered also with mats leaveing a Seperation in the whole length of about 12 or 15 inches wide, left for
the purpose of admitting light and for the Smok of the fire to pass which is made in the middle of the house."*

WILLIAM CLARK, October 17, 1805

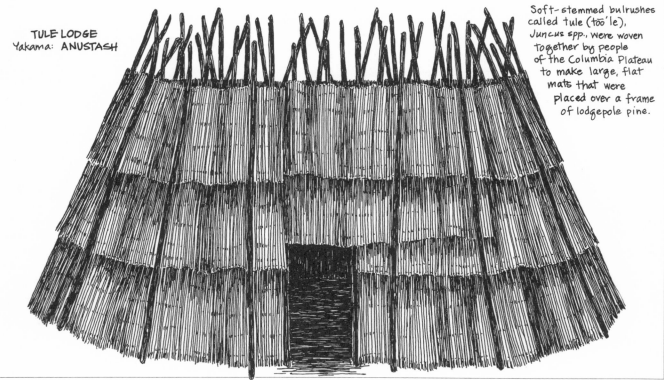

TULE LODGE
Yakama: ANUSTASH

Soft-stemmed bulrushes
called tule (tōō'le),
Juncus spp., were woven
together by people
of the Columbia Plateau
to make large, flat
mats that were
placed over a frame
of lodgepole pine.

OH, JOY!

After leaving the Nez Perce, the expedition witnessed a dramatic change of landscape. Abrupt hillsides covered with towering ponderosa pine opened out to rolling, starkly barren hills, which in turn became a broad sagebrush plain. The Clearwater River sped them along to the Snake River, and soon they arrived at the junction of the Snake and Columbia rivers. While traveling down these waterways, the corps encountered many tribes of Native Americans, including relatives of the Nez Perce: the Yakamas, Wanapams, and Walla Wallas. Although they were not long among these groups, Captain Lewis, as usual, took time to record their basic vocabularies. The corps relied on the native people for food, trading with them to acquire a variety of local staples—mainly dried salmon, roots, nuts, and berries. They also purchased dogs to supplement their diet; many of the expedition members preferred dog meat to fish.

Passing deeper into the Columbia River Gorge, the scenery changed again—from treeless, semidesert hills to lofty, forest-covered mountainsides.

"SW. 14 miles to a rock... resembling a hat just below a rapid"
WILLIAM CLARK
October 19, 1805

HAT ROCK
Hat Rock State Park, OR
↑ 100' top to "brim" ↓

ROUND HAT
of 1803 infantry uniform

↑ to 120' ↓
BIGLEAF MAPLE

↑ to 200' ↓
DOUGLAS-FIR

↑ to 20' ↓
VINE MAPLE

Oh, Joy!

Oh, joy!
Ocean in view,
Ocean in view—
Can it be true?
We've traveled and we've labored,
We've seen the country through,
And now we've great joy with the ocean in view!

At Beacon Rock the first tidewater was noticed, and in just a few days, on November 7, 1805, Captain Clark wrote in his field journal, "Ocian in view! O! the joy!" Although he was mistaken (it was actually the broad Columbia River estuary), they would very soon reach the goal that they had been in pursuit of for eighteen long months.

"Great joy in camp we are in view of the Ocian...this great Pacific Ocean which we been so long anxious to See. and the roreing or noise made by the waves braking on the rockey Shores (as I suppose) may be heard disti[n]ctly"
WILLIAM CLARK
November 7, 1805

"at 4 oClock PM the wind Shifted about to the S.W. and blew with great violence imediately from the Ocean for about two hours, notwithstanding the disagreeable Situation of our party all wet and cold (and one which they have experienced for Several days past) they are chearfull and anxious to See further into the Ocian"

WILLIAM CLARK
November 9, 1805

"I directed all the men who wished to see more of the main Ocian to prepare themselves to Set out with me early on tomorrow morning."

WILLIAM CLARK
November 17, 1805

"men appear much Satisfied with their trip beholding with estonishment the high waves dashing against the rocks & this emence Ocian"

WILLIAM CLARK
November 18, 1805

"a moderate rain the greater part of the last night, Cap! Lewis Branded a tree with his name Date &c. I marked my name the Day & year on a alder tree, the party all Cut the first letters of their names on different trees in the bottom."

WILLIAM CLARK
November 23, 1805

"this Cape is an ellivated circlier [circular] point covered with thick timber on the iner Side and open grassey exposur next to the Sea... this cape as also the Shore both on the Bay & Sea coast is a dark brown rock."

WILLIAM CLARK, November 18, 1805

(WA)

Cape Disappointment

Columbia River

PACIFIC OCEAN

(OR)

US Cap.ᵗ M. Lewis

CAPTAIN LEWIS'S BRAND
Used to mark trees and belongings. (Lewis's branding iron was found in the late 1800s near The Dalles, OR.)

CAPE DISAPPOINTMENT, Ilwaco, WA
Named by British fur trader John Meares in 1788 when he was unable to locate the Columbia River.

Along with geographic changes, Lewis and Clark noted major differences in the lifestyles of Native Americans as the expedition grew closer to the ocean. Villages of cedar plank houses—the first wooden houses they had seen in months—began to appear at river's edge. The language changed too, from Sahaptian, used by the Nez Perce and people of the Plateau, to Chinookan. Household articles such as clothing, kettles, and buttons began to show evidence of European trade ships conducting business on the coast. The main mode of travel shifted as well, from horse to canoe. The captains were especially impressed with the fine construction of these canoes and the variety of styles. They were also amazed at the dexterity of the native people in navigating their craft through turbulent water.

CEDAR-PLANK HOUSE

"The Clatsops Chinnooks &c construct their Houses of timber altogether. they are from 14 to 20 feet wide, and from 20 to 60 feet in length, and accomodate one or more families"

WILLIAM CLARK, January 18, 1806

HIGH PROW CANOE ← approx. 21' →

(Fort Clatsop National Memorial, Astoria, OR)

Cathlamet UTILITY CANOE ← 15', 5" →

(Columbia River Maritime Museum, Astoria, OR)

Canoes Remarkably Neat

"the natives inhabiting the lower portion of the Columbia River make their canoes remarkably neat light and well addapted for riding high waves."

MERIWETHER LEWIS, February 1, 1806

Lewis and Clark described (and sketched) four different types of canoes in use on the Lower Columbia River: the utility, high prow, freight, and image canoes. They included drawings of two paddle designs—one, diamond shaped, the other, notched.

↑ approx. 4½' ↓

CANOE PADDLES
Chinook: IS-ICK

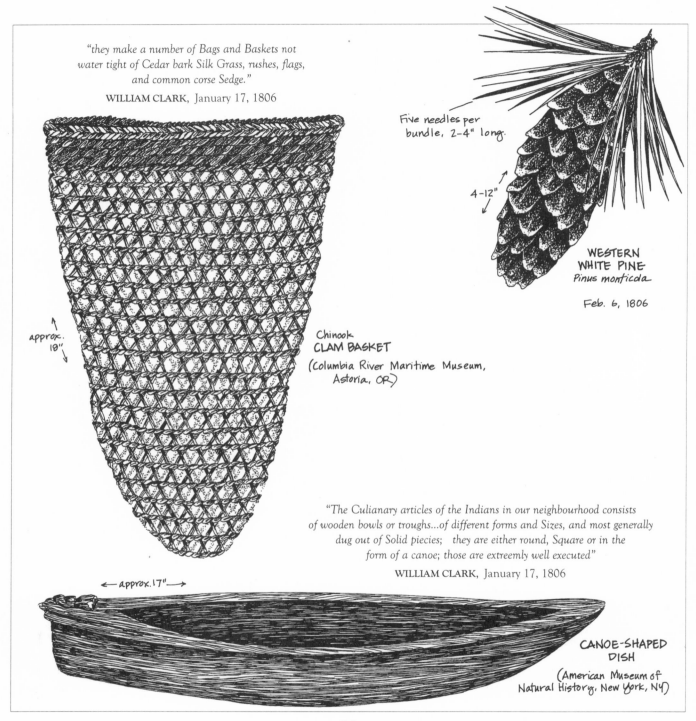

"they make a number of Bags and Baskets not water tight of Cedar bark Silk Grass, rushes, flags, and common corse Sedge."

WILLIAM CLARK, January 17, 1806

Five needles per bundle, 2–4" long.

4–12"

WESTERN WHITE PINE
Pinus monticola

Feb. 6, 1806

approx. 18"

Chinook
CLAM BASKET

(Columbia River Maritime Museum, Astoria, OR)

"The Culianary articles of the Indians in our neighbourhood consists of wooden bowls or troughs...of different forms and Sizes, and most generally dug out of Solid piecies;   they are either round, Square or in the form of a canoe; those are extreemly well executed"

WILLIAM CLARK, January 17, 1806

← approx. 17" →

CANOE-SHAPED DISH

(American Museum of Natural History, New York, NY)

FORT CLATSOP

With winter fast approaching, the Corps of Discovery did not delay in determining possible fort locations. They had three options: remain on the north side of the Columbia, explore the south side of the river for suitability, or return upstream. The captains took a vote—a vote in which all members participated. The party chose to go to the Columbia's southern shore where, according to local Indians, elk were more abundant. Because of their large size in comparison to deer, elk would provide more meat; their hides would better supply the corps with much-needed clothing and moccasins.

On December 7, they found a "most eligible Situation," and the construction of winter quarters soon commenced.

Fort Clatsop

Fort Clatsop was their home
One hundred and six days,
Waiting for springtime
When they could make their way
Back home to the East
To tell what they had done
And heard and witnessed
To Mr. Jefferson.

The rain went on and on and on
Through the winter of that year,
Of the twelve days that were dry
Only six were bright and clear.
The rain went on and on and on,
Those were long and dreary days,
Working at the fort
In busy, quiet ways.

They made elkskin clothes and moccasins,
And candles for their light
To see while writing journals
On dark and cheerless nights.
They traded with the Indians
For whom the fort was named,
Woven hats and berries,
Fish and roots and game.

Clatsop **DOUBLE-BLADED KNIFE**
(Fort Clatsop National Memorial, Astoria, OR)

15" approx.

"the place Cap.t Lewis had viewed...is on a rise about 30 feet higher than the high tides leavel and thickly Covered with lofty pine. this is certainly the most eligable Situation for our purposes of any in its neighbourhood."

WILLIAM CLARK
December 7, 1805

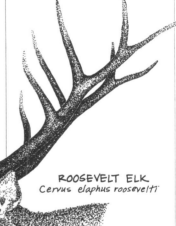

ROOSEVELT ELK
Cervus elaphus roosevelti

"This evening we had what I call an excellent supper it consisted of a marrowbone a piece and a brisket of boiled Elk that had the appearance of a little fat on it. this for Fort Clatsop is living in high stile."
MERIWETHER LEWIS, February 7, 1806

"We completed the building of our huts, 7 in number, all but the covering, which I now find will not be so difficult as I expected; as we have found a kind of timber in plenty, which splits freely, and makes the finest puncheons I have ever seen."

PATRICK GASS
December 14, 1805

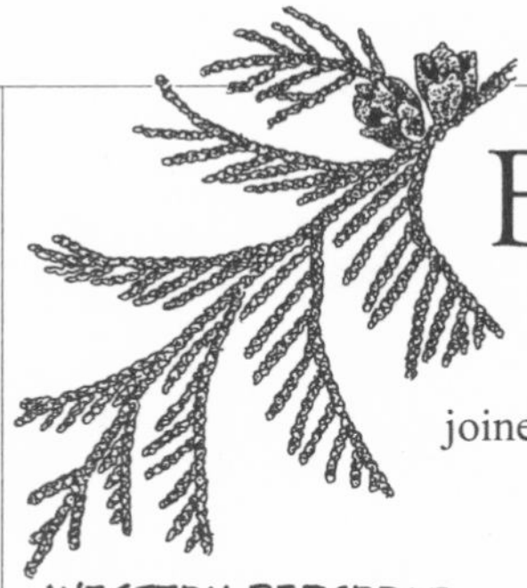

WESTERN REDCEDAR
Thuja plicata
Scale-like foliage; cones ½" long.

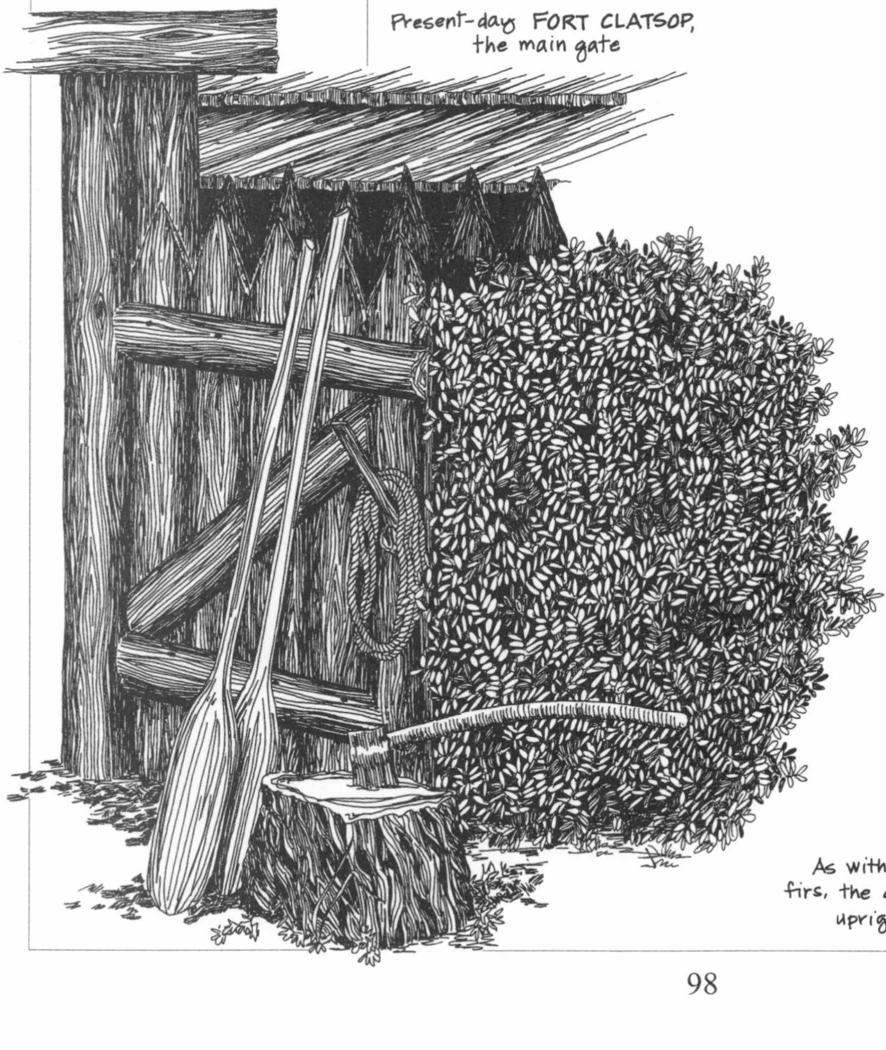

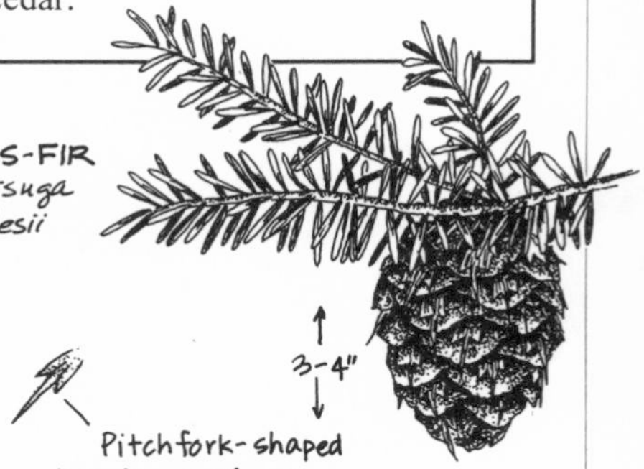

Built in a thick growth of "lofty pine," Fort Clatsop served as a comfortable refuge during the unceasingly wet, stormy months that followed. It stood fifty feet square, with a row of cabins on each side separated by a parade ground. Gated stockade walls joined the two ends. For better defense, the cabin roofs sloped inward; high outer walls prevented intruders from slipping in undetected. In a little over three weeks, Fort Clatsop was complete.

Timber in Plenty

Finding lumber to build the fort was not difficult. A dense forest of towering evergreens grew in the vicinity, including grand fir, Douglas-fir, Sitka spruce, western hemlock, and western redcedar.

Present-day FORT CLATSOP, the main gate

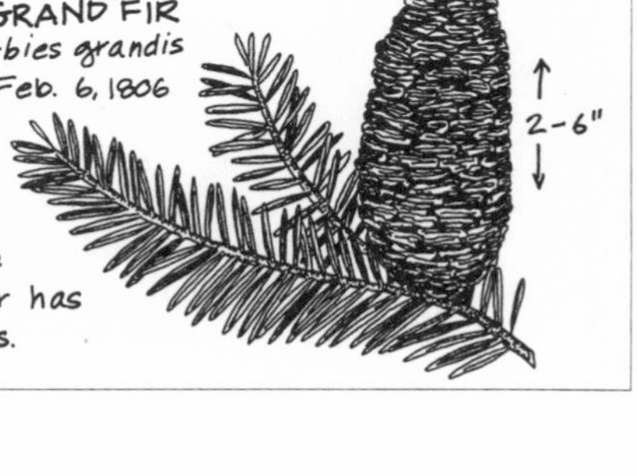

3-4"
Pitchfork-shaped bracts provide easy identification.

DOUGLAS-FIR
Pseudotsuga menziesii

2-6"

GRAND FIR
Abies grandis
Feb. 6, 1806

As with all true firs, the grand fir has upright cones.

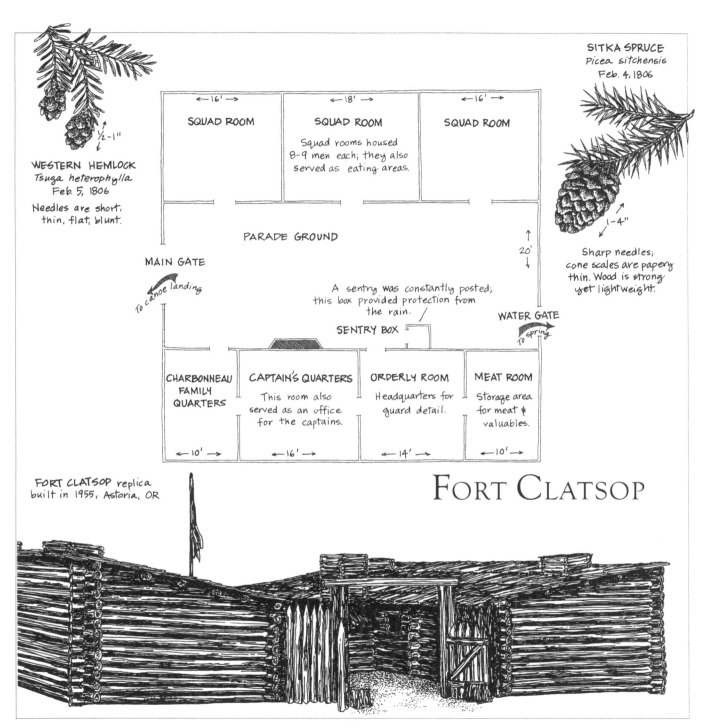

WESTERN HEMLOCK
Tsuga heterophylla
Feb. 5, 1806

Needles are short, thin, flat, blunt.

½ - 1"

SITKA SPRUCE
Picea sitchensis
Feb. 4, 1806

1 - 4"

Sharp needles; cone scales are papery thin. Wood is strong yet lightweight.

← 16' → SQUAD ROOM

← 18' → SQUAD ROOM

Squad rooms housed 8-9 men each; they also served as eating areas.

← 16' → SQUAD ROOM

PARADE GROUND

20'

MAIN GATE

To canoe landing

A sentry was constantly posted; this box provided protection from the rain.

SENTRY BOX

WATER GATE

To spring

CHARBONNEAU FAMILY QUARTERS

← 10' →

CAPTAIN'S QUARTERS

This room also served as an office for the captains.

← 16' →

ORDERLY ROOM

Headquarters for guard detail.

← 14' →

MEAT ROOM

Storage area for meat & valuables.

← 10' →

FORT CLATSOP replica built in 1955, Astoria, OR

FORT CLATSOP

Amply Provided
"They made elkskin clothes and moccasins..."

During the Fort Clatsop winter, the hunters brought in over 130 elk and 20 deer. The process they used for tanning hides—brain tanning—may have been learned from the Mandans a year earlier. Using a scraping tool, the flesh, hair, and fat were removed from the hide as quickly as possible. Next, the hide was soaked in water for about an hour. Then it was spread with the mashed, boiled brains of the animal, rolled, and left to set for several days. The following (and most difficult) step was to soften the hide by stretching and beating it until dry; stopping prematurely would cause the hide to harden. To finish the process, the hide was smoked until brown, which would preserve it against moisture.

The leather was then stitched into clothing. Sergeant Gass recorded that with "great labor" they produced well over 300 pairs of moccasins—enough to amply supply each member of the party.

KNIFE with ELK ANTLER HANDLE

(Fort Clatsop National Memorial, Astoria, OR)

12"

Two-piece, Plains-style MOCCASINS

ELKSKIN SHIRT & OVERALLS

"...and candles for their light"

The long winter on the Pacific Coast would have been even more difficult had the Corps of Discovery not been able to replenish their candle supply. Through dark days and even darker nights, work by candlelight steadily continued.

To make candles, elk fat was boiled with water for several hours to render it. The resulting liquid, clear and amber colored, was then cooled slightly, strained, and poured into prepared molds.

CANDLE MOLD, ready for pouring

sticks keep wick centered & tight

ELKSKIN CAPOTE with elk antler buttons

Buckskin clothing was sometimes fringed to promote drying by draining away moisture.

"this evening we exhausted the last of our candles, but fortunately had taken the precaution to bring with us moulds and wick, by means of which and some Elk's tallow in our possession we do not yet consider ourselves destitute of this necessary article"

MERIWETHER LEWIS
January 13, 1806

Leather garments created by corps members were probably patterned after the military-style clothing worn when the expedition began. Overalls were snug, shoe-length breeches. Shirts may have been loose pullovers, fashioned with a deep slit in the front; they may also have been designed after the two-hide shirt worn by Native Americans. Capotes were large overgarments, extending to the knees and usually outfitted with a hood. Typically made of woolen blankets, these military-issue coats were popular with French *voyageurs*, Native Americans, and frontiersmen. Moccasins may have been sewn Plains-style, using a two-piece pattern, with heavy leather forming the soles and lighter or middleweight leather, the tops.

Purchased of the Clatsops
"They traded with the Indians..."

Most of the trade between expedition members and their neighbors was to obtain food. Because the corps's regular fare was almost exclusively elk, the roots, berries, fish, and whale blubber they purchased provided a refreshing change.

A variety of roots were brought to the fort for trade, including thistle, fern, cattail, and horsetail. Wapato, a root which grew in swampy areas several miles upstream, was especially prized by the native people. It soon became a valued staple for the corps as well.

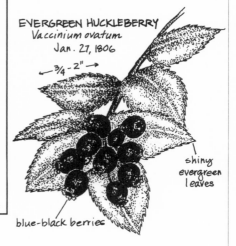

actual size

Sagitta means "arrow"; wapato has arrowhead-shaped leaves.

WAPATO ROOT
Sagittaria latifolia
An aquatic plant; potato-like tubers were prepared by roasting, boiling & drying.

Berry types included evergreen huckleberry, salal, and bearberry. Northwest Coast natives preserved salal berries and evergreen huckleberries by drying them in the form of large loaves. To serve, the loaves were broken and reconstituted with water to create a soup.

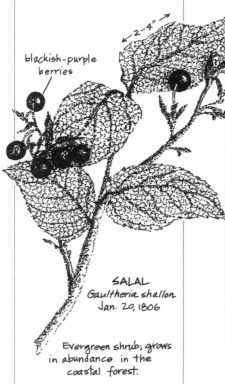

blackish-purple berries

2-4"

SALAL
Gaultheria shallon
Jan. 20, 1806

Evergreen shrub; grows in abundance in the coastal forest.

By the time the Corps of Discovery reached the Pacific Ocean, their supply of trade goods was woefully depleted. Remaining items included fish hooks, ribbon, pieces of brass, beads, and small tools. On January 6, 1806, Captain Lewis wrote, "our merchandize is reduced to a mear handful." With the rest of winter and a long return journey ahead, they worked desperately to bolster the dwindling stock. Corps members began to offer personal belongings and clothing for trade. They even transformed their large flag into five robes for bartering.

EVERGREEN HUCKLEBERRY
Vaccinium ovatum
Jan. 27, 1806

3/4-2"

shiny evergreen leaves

blue-black berries

A favored type of fish purchased by the corps was the eulachon or "candlefish." Cooking them as the Clatsops did—which was to roast a number of fish together on a spit, without any preparation—yielded the tastiest results. Captain Clark described the eulachon as "delicate and lussious."

One nonfood item that drew special attention from the captains was the cone-shaped, nearly waterproof Clatsop hat. This style was produced by many of the Northwest Coast tribes and was often decorated with ocean-themed designs. Clatsop hats were made of cedar bark (gathered locally) and decorated with beargrass (obtained from inland tribes); a string under the chin held the hat in place. The explorers were so impressed with the design and workmanship of these tightly woven head coverings that they purchased several.

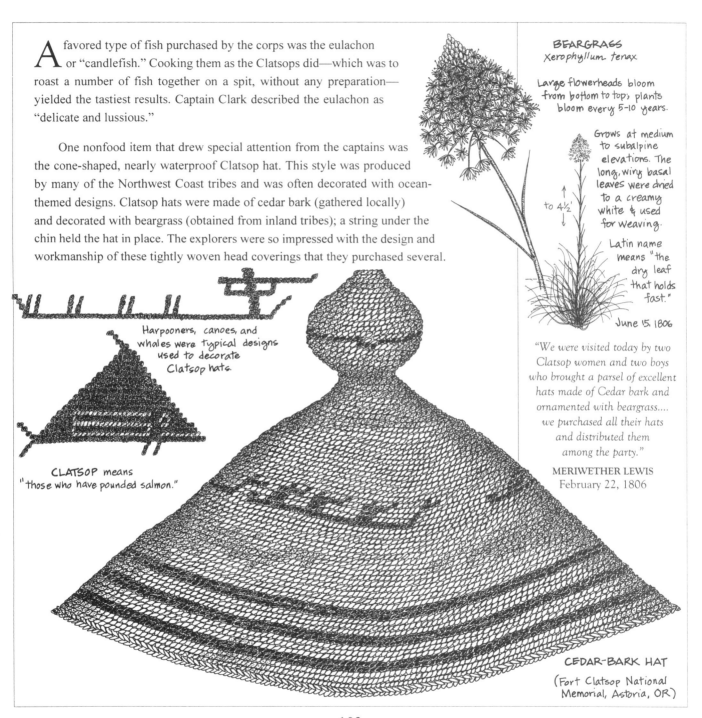

BEARGRASS
Xerophyllum tenax

Large flowerheads bloom from bottom to top; plants bloom every 5-10 years.

Grows at medium to subalpine elevations. The long, wiry basal leaves were dried to a creamy white & used for weaving.

to 4½'

Latin name means "the dry leaf that holds fast."

June 15, 1806

Harpooners, canoes, and whales were typical designs used to decorate Clatsop hats.

CLATSOP means "those who have pounded salmon."

"We were visited today by two Clatsop women and two boys who brought a parsel of excellent hats made of Cedar bark and ornamented with beargrass.... we purchased all their hats and distributed them among the party."

MERIWETHER LEWIS
February 22, 1806

CEDAR-BARK HAT
(Fort Clatsop National Memorial, Astoria, OR)

Busily Employed
"...working at the fort in busy, quiet ways"

Time at the fort passed slowly, but with a steady flow of activity.

Hunters struggled through dense forest underbrush to maintain an adequate meat supply. Others worked at camp, cooking and preserving what was brought in—either by jerking (nearly impossible in high humidity) or smoking. Because of the wet climate, meat had to be dealt with quickly or it would spoil—and often it did.

Another ongoing task was the tending of fires. In addition to providing warmth, fires were needed to cook, smoke meat and hides, melt lead for bullets, and render fat for candles. Listed as part of the camp equipment purchased for the expedition were 30 "Steels for striking or making fire" and 100 "Flints for making fire." Although the men were undoubtedly experts at starting fires with flint and steel, it must have been extremely difficult to maintain dry tinder and wood in the continual rain.

The SALT WORKS Recreated in Seaside, OR

About fifteen miles southwest of the fort (away from the influence of fresh water from the Columbia River), another time-consuming chore was taking place: the boiling down of salt-water to build up a much-needed salt supply. Using five large kettles, the men assigned to this task could produce three quarts to a gallon of salt per day. What a treat for the corps to be able to salt their meat again!

While looking after day-to-day requirements, the corps kept an eye on what might be needed for the journey home. Replacement clothing was tucked away. Gunpowder, which had been stored in tightly sealed lead canisters, was inventoried and examined for dryness; the small amount that had become wet was set out to dry. The canoes were made ready, and elkskin coverings were prepared to protect baggage.

LEAD GUNPOWDER CANISTER

Each tightly stoppered, wax-sealed canister held enough gunpowder to fire the lead from which it was made. Fifty-two canisters were recorded on the list of supplies purchased for the expedition.

LEAD BULLETS

sprue

BULLET MOLD

Melted lead was poured into a mold to form bullets. After being released from the mold, the bullets were trimmed of the sprue.

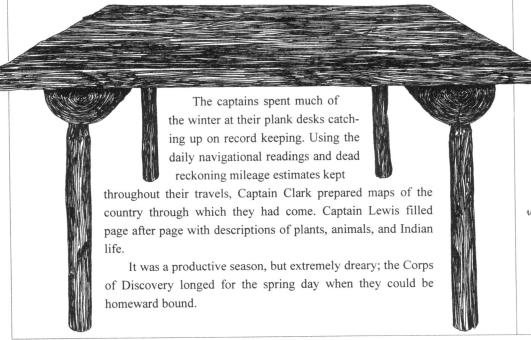

The captains spent much of the winter at their plank desks catching up on record keeping. Using the daily navigational readings and dead reckoning mileage estimates kept throughout their travels, Captain Clark prepared maps of the country through which they had come. Captain Lewis filled page after page with descriptions of plants, animals, and Indian life.

It was a productive season, but extremely dreary; the Corps of Discovery longed for the spring day when they could be homeward bound.

"I compleated a map of the Countrey through which we have been passing from the Mississippi at the Mouth of Missouri to this place."
WILLIAM CLARK
February 14, 1806

"no movement of the party today worthy of notice. every thing moves on in the old way and we are counting the days which seperate us from the 1st of April and which bind us to fort Clatsop."
MERIWETHER LEWIS
March 3, 1806

When the Lewis and Clark Expedition left Fort Clatsop on March 23, 1806, the road ahead was long but for the most part familiar. They knew where they were going and what to expect. They would again have to reckon with the Columbia River rapids. Food would be hard to find. The Bitterroots—those beautiful, formidable Bitterroots— would have to be crossed one more time.

Traveling up the Columbia *was* grueling. Unending rain and troublesome relations with many of the Native Americans made the task even more difficult. At the Long Narrows they traded for enough horses to travel overland to the Nez Perce villages. Although they were anxious to press on, lingering snow in the Bitterroots caused them to delay among the Nez Perce for several weeks. At last the day came when they could resume their trek. The snow was still deep, but it was firm, and with competent Nez Perce guides to direct them they made it safely to Traveler's Rest.

At this point the expedition divided. Clark, with the Charbonneau family and several others, headed southeast through Shoshoni country to the Yellowstone River, then on to the Missouri River. Lewis, with a smaller detachment, would follow a Nez Perce trail to Great Falls, then go north to explore the Marias River area. It was during this time that the expedition's most serious Indian conflict occurred. Lewis and three of his men (George Drouillard, Joseph Field, and Reubin Field) had spent the night camped with a small party of "Minnetares of the North"—Blackfeet or Gros Ventres of the Prairie. At dawn they awoke to find the Indians absconding with their rifles and horses. A fight ensued. One of the Indians was killed and another critically, probably fatally, wounded. Fearing another confrontation, Lewis and his men rode at breakneck speed to the Missouri River where, to their "unspeakable satisfaction," they met other members of their detachment arriving in canoes. They released the horses, boarded the canoes, and proceeded down the river with the hope of soon overtaking Clark's group.

LEWIS'S
WILD FLAX
Linum lewisii

July 9, 1806

Sky blue
flowers on
delicate
stems;
blossoms
last only
for one day.

↑
200'
↓

POMPEYS PILLAR
Billings, MT

Wm Clark
July 25th, 1806

Captain Clark named it
"Pompy's Tower" after
Sacagawea's son. He etched
his name and the date in
the sandstone—his
inscription can still be
seen today.

THEY PLIED THEIR OARS WELL

On August 12, 1806, the separated parties were safely rejoined on the Missouri River. With the wind and the current in their favor, the corps was able to enjoy another happy reunion two days later with their friends at the Mandan and Hidatsa villages. After stopping there for a few days, they bid farewell to the Charbonneau family and Private John Colter (all of whom were discharged) and began the final stretch of the expedition.

Anxiety to get home as quickly as possible was intense. It is not hard to sympathize: The last miles of an extended trip are always the longest. For the Corps of Discovery it was no different.

COUGAR
Felis concolor

Also known as
MOUNTAIN LION
and PANTHER

They Plied Their Oars Well

They plied their oars well, so anxious to tell
Country and friends where they'd been;
The Missouri's current now on their side,
Chances were good they'd see home again,
Chances were good they'd see home.

Exchanging leather for linen shirts with traders going upstream,
Imagining what the reception would be, into the oars they leaned—

They plied their oars well, miles quickly sailed,
Voices in harmony sang;
The Missouri's current now on their side,
Chances were good they'd see home again,
Chances were good they'd see home.

Provisions low meant stopping to hunt, but hunting would take too much time;
The party, eager to push to the end, said livin' on pawpaws was fine!

They plied their oars well, glad hearts did swell
When landmarks familiar were seen;
The Missouri's current now on their side,
Chances were good they'd see home again,
Chances were good they'd see home.

The sight of cows at river's edge made a shout to be raised for joy;
With the thought of civilization ahead, all might and main were employed—

They plied their oars well, for they had not failed,
Accomplishment prodded them on;
The Missouri's current now on their side,
Chances were good they'd see home again,
Chances were good they'd see home.

The Missouri's current now on their side,
In just a short while they'd be home.

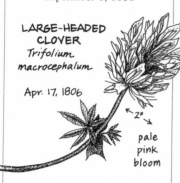

LARGE-HEADED
CLOVER
Trifolium macrocephalum

Apr. 17, 1806

← 2" →

pale
pink
bloom

The Wish of the Party
"so anxious to tell..."

Because the journals repeatedly describe the mood of the expedition as they descended the Missouri, it is not hard to imagine the thoughts that must have been turning over and over in their minds. They had been gone for twenty-eight months—longer than many had originally expected. Excitement to once again see family and friends would have certainly been mixed with apprehension. Were parents still living? Had the "best girl" waited, or had she given up and married another? What kind of reception would they receive as they once again entered civilization? What would life be like after such an adventure?

They must have been bursting at the seams with stories to share with their loved ones. They had seen many strange and wonderful sights, witnessed creatures curious and beautiful. Picture the thrill of describing the White Cliffs of the Missouri or the grandeur of the Rockies to someone who had never been further than forty miles from his eastern United States home. What fun it would be to entertain wide-eyed children with accounts of "barking squirrels" and rattlesnakes, buffalo hunts and bear escapades. They could tell of Native Americans whose lives were vastly different from the lives of those at home—of people who lived in houses made of earth, or who flattened their foreheads as a sign of high social status, or who could navigate raging rivers in finely crafted canoes.

There were sobering memories to relate as well, of illness and danger, of near starvation, of the one man who didn't make it home. They had all had brushes with death; each accompanying tale was worthy of legend.

With the accomplishment of a successful expedition behind them and the unknown beckoning them forward, it is no wonder that the party was "extreamly anxious to get on."

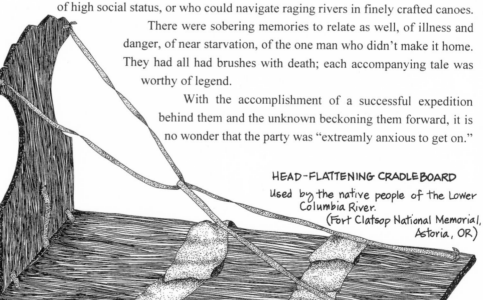

HEAD-FLATTENING CRADLEBOARD
Used by the native people of the Lower Columbia River.
(Fort Clatsop National Memorial, Astoria, OR)

With Great Velocity
"miles quickly sailed..."

Returning from the Mandan village to St. Louis took about a month. Two years earlier that same distance (but rowing *against* the current) took over five months. For Captain Clark even one month was too long. When recording the miles covered each day he frequently betrayed his disappointment:

"we came 52 miles to day only with a head wind."
"haveing made 73 miles only to day."
"haveing decended only 53 miles to day."

Home just couldn't come fast enough.

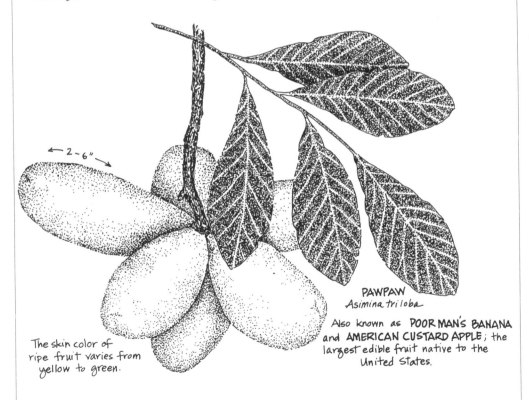

← 2 - 6" →

The skin color of ripe fruit varies from yellow to green.

PAWPAW
Asimina triloba
Also known as **POOR MAN'S BANANA** and **AMERICAN CUSTARD APPLE**; the largest edible fruit native to the United States.

"our party entirely out of provisions subsisting on poppaws. we divide[d] the buiskit which amounted to nearly one buisket per man, this in addition to the poppaws is to last us down to the Settlement's which is 150 miles the party appear perfectly contented and tell us that they can live very well on the pappaws."
WILLIAM CLARK
September 18, 1806

"the men plyd their oares & we decended with great velocity, only came too once for the purpose of gathering pappows, our anxiety as also the wish of the party to proceed on as expeditiously as possible to the Illinois enduce us to continue on without halting to hunt."
WILLIAM CLARK
September 19, 1806

"the party being extreemly anxious to get down ply their ores very well, we saw some cows on the bank which was a joyfull Sight to the party and caused a Shout to be raised for joy"
WILLIAM CLARK
September 20, 1806

Robinson Crusoes

"They really have the appearance of Robinson Crusoes–dressed entirely in buckskins."
ST. LOUIS RESIDENT, September 23, 1806

The returning Corps of Discovery had a dramatically different appearance than the group of adventurers that had set out from St. Louis in 1804. Endless hours in the sun had baked light-colored skin to a deep brown. Military clothing, worn out long before, had been replaced with clothes made of buckskin. Rough-hewn dugout canoes—durable, but not nearly so grand as the keelboat—now transported the men through the snags and sand bars of the Missouri. Their load of cargo was reduced to only what was essential, much of it stored in lightweight rawhide sacks, Native American fashion.

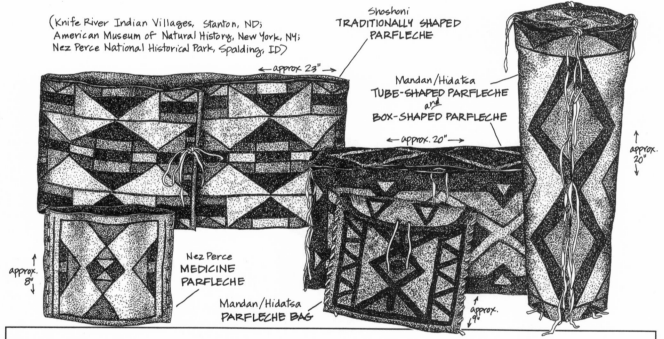

(Knife River Indian Villages, Stanton, ND; American Museum of Natural History, New York, NY; Nez Perce National Historical Park, Spalding, ID)

Shoshoni
TRADITIONALLY SHAPED PARFLECHE

Mandan/Hidatsa
TUBE-SHAPED PARFLECHE
and
BOX-SHAPED PARFLECHE

← approx. 23" →

← approx. 20" →

↑ approx. 20" ↓

Nez Perce
MEDICINE PARFLECHE

↑ approx. 8" ↓

Mandan/Hidatsa
PARFLECHE BAG

↑ approx. 9" ↓

Made of thin, stiff rawhide in a variety of shapes and sizes, parfleches were used to store food, clothing, personal items, and other household goods. The outside of a parfleche was decorated with outlined geometric designs, usually in red, blue, black, green, yellow, and brown. Paint was made from mineral and plant materials mixed with water and egg yolk.

"roots of three different kinds...were foalded in as many parchment hides of buffaloe."
MERIWETHER LEWIS, August 22, 1805

To use a traditionally shaped (also called envelope) parfleche, the long top and bottom edges were folded in toward the center, covering the contents. The sides were folded in next, overlapping. To secure the bundle, laces were pulled through the lacing holes and tied.

BACK HOME

What an adventure it had been! They had suffered, but endured. They had struggled, but overcome. And now, at last, the story of their amazing journey could be shared with Thomas Jefferson and the waiting folks at home.

Back Home

The end of the journey!
They'd been gone so long
Folks back home were thinking surely something had gone wrong.
Missouri River traders called them men returned from graves,
For rumors were that they'd been killed
Or taken in as slaves.

Though many U.S. folks had given up on their return,
There was one who still had hope: Mr. Jefferson.
His dream had surely been fulfilled—
The wealth of knowledge gained
Was all that he had hoped for
And soon would be explained.

All St. Louis greeted them when they arrived in town;
The corps presented their salute by firing off three rounds.
Celebrations welcomed them,
Newspapers spread their name,
Towns of happy citizens
Declared the corps's fame.

The journey was now ended,
The story just begun,
There'd be changes to our land because of what they'd done.
The captains and their party
Rejoiced to be back home—
The adventure was over,
But the tale had just begun.

WILD HYACINTH
Brodiaea grandiflora
Apr. 20, 1806

pale blue blooms

Bulbs valued by native people for food.

↑ to 30" ↓

"this Gentleman informed us that we had been long Since given out [up] by the people of the US Generaly and almost forgotton, the President of the U. States had yet hopes of us"
WILLIAM CLARK
September 17, 1806

"every person, both French and americans seem to express great pleasure at our return, and acknowledged themselves much astonished in seeing us return. they informed us that we were supposed to have been lost long since, and were entirely given out by every person &c."
WILLIAM CLARK
September 20, 1806

"about 12 oClock we arived in Site of St. Louis fired three Rounds as we approached...the people gathred on the Shore and Huzzared three cheers....the party all considerable much rejoiced that we have the Expedition Completed and now we...entend to return to our native homes to See our parents once more as we have been So long from them."
JOHN ORDWAY
September 23, 1806

AFTER THE JOURNEY

Following the expedition, many of the corps members remained in the military. Others returned to farming; several went into the fur trade. Although the fate of some members is unknown and many had passed away by 1828, a few of the men went on to lead colorful lives. John Colter was a trapper and explorer. He is credited as being the first white man to see what is now the Yellowstone National Park area. Patrick Gass fought in the War of 1812 and lived to the age of 98. Alexander Willard also lived a long life: He died in California at age 87. George Shannon became a lawyer, a judge, and a Missouri state senator.

For their service on the expedition, enlisted corps members were each compensated with double pay and 320 acres of land. Captain Lewis petitioned for them in a letter to Secretary of War Henry Dearborn:

"With respect to all those persons whose names are entered on this roll, I feel a peculiar pleasure in declaring, that the ample support which they gave me under every difficulty; the manly firmness which they evinced on every necessary occasion; and the patience and fortitude with which they submitted to, and bore, the fatigues and painful sufferings incident to my late tour to the Pacific Ocean, entitles them to my warmest approbation and thanks; nor will I suppress the expression of a hope, that the recollection of services, thus faithfully performed, will meet a just reward, in an ample remuneration on the part of our Government."

In addition to double pay, the captains each received 1,600 acres of land. They also received appointments to new positions—Lewis as governor of the Territory of Louisiana, Clark as superintendent of Indian affairs for the Territory of Louisiana. Honors were showered upon them for their accomplishments by officials and citizenry alike. In his message to Congress on December 2, 1806, President Jefferson said,

"it is but justice to say that Messrs. Lewis and Clarke, and their brave companions, have by this arduous service deserved well of their country."

violet-blue flowers

↑ 1–3' ↓

July 5, 1806

WESTERN BLUE FLAG
Iris missouriensis

112

In an address to the captains on behalf of the citizens of Fincastle, Virginia, the chairman, Pat Lockhart, declared,

> *"esteem and gratitude induce us to offer you our sincere*
> *congratulations, upon your safe return to the bosom of your country....*
> *you have extended the knowledge of the Geography of your country; in other respects*
> *enriched Science; and opened to the United States a source of inexhaustable wealth...*
> *You have uniformly respected the rights of humanity,*
> *actuated by principles of genuine philanthropy...*
> *We concieve it to be a signal proof of the wisdom and attention with which you have*
> *conducted the expedition, that but one man has been lost to your country."*

Captain Clark responded,

> *"It will be a pleasing reflection in future life to find that the expedition has been*
> *productive of those advantages to our Country, Geography, and science...*
> *we ought to assign the general safety of the party to a singular interposition*
> *of providence, and not to the wisdom of those who commanded the expedition....*
> *I will do my self the Honor to hand Cap! Lewis and make known to the*
> *faithfull party that accompanied us your friendly address, which I will*
> *undertake to say for them will be justly appreciated."*

The journals of Lewis and Clark were not officially published until 1814, nearly eight years after the completion of the expedition. This two-volume condensed narrative is often referred to as the Biddle-Allen edition after its editors, Nicholas Biddle and Paul Allen. Within the next several years a number of condensed versions were published in Europe, including a three-volume Dutch translation. In the mid-1800s the journals were again published in the United States in a smaller format known as the Harper's Edition.

The journals were printed in their entirety for the first time in 1904-1905. Edited by Reuben Gold Thwaites, this eight-volume edition was the most complete collection of the journals until the late twentieth century. At that time a comprehensive thirteen-volume work, edited by Gary Moulton, was published by the University of Nebraska Press.

In addition to the Thwaites and Moulton volumes, several condensed versions of the journals of Lewis and Clark are available today by editors such as Elliot Coues (first published in the late nineteenth century), Frank Bergon, John Bakeless, and Bernard DeVoto (published in the twentieth century). Also available are the journals of Patrick Gass (first published in 1807), John Ordway, Joseph Whitehouse, and Charles Floyd.

fragrant yellow blooms

July 6, 1806

ANTELOPE BRUSH
Purshia tridentata

Also known as
BITTERBRUSH

Bibliography

Ambrose, Stephen E. *Undaunted Courage: Meriwether Lewis, Thomas Jefferson, and the Opening of the American West.* New York: Simon & Schuster, 1996.

————. *Lewis & Clark: Voyage of Discovery.* Washington, DC: National Geographic Society, 1998.

Anderson, Irving W. "The Sacagawea Mystique: Her Age, Name, Role and Final Destiny." *Columbia,* vol. 13, no. 3 (Fall 1999).

Burroughs, Raymond Darwin. *The Natural History of the Lewis and Clark Expedition.* East Lansing: Michigan State University Press, 1961.

Caduto, Micheal J. and Joseph Bruchac. *Native American Gardening: Stories, Projects and Recipes for Families.* Golden, CO: Fulcrum Publishing, 1996.

Carrick, Micheal. "Lewis & Clark: Question & Answer." *Oregon Chapter Lewis and Clark Trail Heritage Foundation Newsletter,* vol. 4, no. 11 (June 2002).

Charbonneau, Louis. "Seaman's Trail: Fact vs. Fiction." *We Proceeded On,* vol. 15, no. 4 (November 1989).

Chuinard, Eldon G. *Only One Man Died: Medical Aspects of the Lewis and Clark Expedition.* Glendale, CA: Arthur Clark Co., 1980.

Cous, Elliot, ed. *The History of the Lewis and Clark Expedition.* New York: Dover, 1987; reprint of Francis P. Harper 4-vol. edition, 1893.

Cutright, Paul Russell. *Lewis and Clark: Pioneering Naturalists.* Lincoln: University of Illinois Press, 1969; reprinted by First Bison Books, 1989.

De Voto, Bernard, ed. *The Journals of Lewis and Clark.* New York: Houghton Mifflin, 1953.

Duncan, Dayton. *Lewis and Clark: An Illustrated History.* New York: Alfred A. Knopf, Inc., 1997.

Ehrlich, Paul; David S. Dobkin; Darryl Wheye. *The Birders Handbook: A Field Guide to the Natural History of North American Birds.* New York: Simon and Schuster, Fireside, 1988.

Gildea, Hugh. "Tracking Down the Trump." *We Proceeded On,* vol. 25, no. 2 (May 1999).

Hitchcock, Charles Leo. *Vascular Plants of the Pacific Northwest.* Seattle: University of Washington Press, 1955-1969.

Holland, Leandra. "Preserving Food on the L & C Expedition." *We Proceeded On,* vol. 27, no. 3 (August 2001).

Hunt, Robert. "Merry to the Fiddle: The Musical Amusement of the Lewis and Clark Party." *We Proceeded On,* vol. 14, no. 4 (November 1988).

Jackson, Donald, ed. *Letters of the Lewis and Clark Expedition, with Related Documents: 1783-1854.* Urbana: University of Illinois Press, 1962.

Jackson, William H. *Picture Maker of the Old West.* New York: Charles Scribner's Sons, 1947.

James, George Wharton. *Indian Basketry & How to Make Baskets.* Glorieta, NM: The Rio Grand Press, Inc., 1970; reprint of 1903 edition.

Jensen, Edward C. and Charles R. Ross. *Trees to Know in Oregon.* Corvallis: Oregon State University, 1994.

Krumm, Bob and James Krumm. *The Pacific Northwest Berry Book.* Helena, MT: Falcon Publishing, Inc., 1998.

Lyons, C.P. *Trees & Shrubs of Washington.* Renton, WA: Lone Pine Publishing, 1999.

————. *Wildflowers of Washington.* Renton, WA: Lone Pine Publishing, 1997.

Marshal, Mel. *Cooking Over Coals.* New York: Winchester Press, 1971.

Miles, Charles. *Indian & Eskimo Artifacts of North America.* New York: Bonama Books, 1963.

Montgomery, David R. *An Illustrated Guide for Making Authentic Indian Clothing, Shelters, and Ornaments.* Bountiful, UT: Horizon Publishing & Distributors, Inc., 1985.

Moore, Bob. "Did the Corps of Discovery Actually Eat Candles?" *We Proceeded On,* vol. 25, no. 2 (May 1999).

———. "Corps of Discovery Hats." *We Proceeded On,* vol. 27, no. 2 (May 2001).

Mosher, Milton M. *Trees of Washington.* Washington State University, Extension Bulletin no. 440, reprinted June 1971.

Moulton, Gary, ed. *The Journals of the Lewis & Clark Expedition.* Lincoln: University of Nebraska Press, 1983-2001.

Mussulman, Joseph A. "The Greatest Harmoney: Meddicine Songs on the Lewis and Clark Trail." *We Proceeded On,* vol. 23, no. 4 (November 1997).

Nell, Donald F. and John E. Taylor. *Lewis and Clark in the Three Rivers Valleys.* Tucson: The Patrice Press, 1996.

O'Conner, Hyla. *The Early American Cookbook.* Englewood Cliffs, NJ: Prentice-Hall, Inc., 1974.

Peterson, Roger Tory. *A Field Guide to Western Birds.* Boston: Houghton Mifflin Company, 1941.

Ronda, James P. *Lewis and Clark among the Indians.* Lincoln: University of Nebraska Press, 1984.

———. "A Most Perfect Harmony: Life at Fort Mandan." *We Proceeded On,* vol. 14, no. 4 (November 1988).

Russell, Carl P. *Firearms, Traps, & Tools of the Mountain Men.* Albuquerque: University of New Mexico Press, 1977; reprint by arrangement with Alfred A. Knopf, Inc.

Salomon, Julian Harris. *Book of Indian Crafts and Indian Lore.* New York: Harper & Row, 1928.

Schlick, Mary Dodds. *Columbia River Basketry: Gift of the Ancestors, Gift of the Earth.* Seattle: University of Washington Press, 1994.

Schmidt, Thomas and Jeremy Schmidt. *The Saga of Lewis & Clark into the Uncharted West.* New York: DK Publishing, 1999.

Schmidt, Thomas. *National Geographic's Guide to the Lewis & Clark Trail.* New York: National Geographic Society, 1998.

Scurlock, William H., ed. *The Book of Buckskinning.* Texarkana, TX: Rebel Publishing Company, 1980.

———. *The Book of Buckskinning II.* Texarkana, TX: Rebel Publishing Company, 1983.

———. *The Book of Buckskinning III.* Texarkana, TX: Rebel Publishing Company, 1985.

———. *The Book of Buckskinning IV.* Texarkana, TX: Rebel Publishing Company, 1987.

———. *The Book of Buckskinning V.* Texarkana, TX: Rebel Publishing Company, 1989.

———. *The Book of Buckskinning VI.* Texarkana, TX: Rebel Publishing Company, 1992.

———. *The Book of Buckskinning VII.* Texarkana, TX: Rebel Publishing Company, 1995.

Sherrow, Victoria. *Indians of the Plateau and Great Basin.* New York: Bentford Books, Inc., 1992.

Skarmeas, Nancy J. "Legendary Americans: Lewis and Clark." *Ideals,* vol. 55, no. 4 (July 1998).

Starr, Eileen. "Celestial Navigation Basics." *We Proceeded On,* vol. 27, no. 4 (November 2001).

Strong, Ruth and Emory Strong. *Seeking Western Waters.* Portland: Oregon Historical Society Press, 1995.

Suttles, Wayne, ed. *Handbook of North American Indians, Volume 7.* Washington, DC: Smithsonian Institution, 1990.

Taylor, Colin F. *Buckskin and Buffalo: The Artistry of the Plains Indians.* New York: Rizzoli, 1998.

Thomas, Davis and Karen Ronnefeldt, ed. *People of the First Man: Life Among the Plains in Their Final Days of Glory/ Watercolors by Karl Bodmer.* New York: E.P. Dutton & Co., Inc., 1963.

Thwaites, Reuben Gold, ed. *Original Journals of the Lewis and Clark Expedition.* New York: Dodd, Mead & Company, 1904-1905; reprint by Digital Scanning, Inc., Scituate, MA, 2001.

Wilber, C. Keith. *Picture Book of the Continental Soldier.* Harrisburg: Stackpole Books, 1969.

Places to Visit

There are countless interesting and beautiful sites along the Lewis and Clark Trail for today's traveler to enjoy, from major interpretive centers to roadside pullouts. The following list is by no means comprehensive.

Jefferson National Expansion Memorial
11 N 4th Street, St. Louis, MO 63102

(314) 655-1700

Emphasis on Thomas Jefferson,
Westward Expansion, Lewis and Clark.

Missouri Historical Society
PO Box 11940, St. Louis, MO 63110-0040

(314) 454-3124

Native cultures, Louisiana Purchase,
Lewis and Clark.

The Lewis and Clark Boathouse and Nature Center
1050 Riverside Drive, St. Charles, MO 63301

(636) 947-3199

Extensive information on Lewis and Clark
with an emphasis on the boats and natural history
of the expedition.

Lewis and Clark State Park
Onawa, IA

(712) 423-2829

Replica keelboat and pirogues.

Sergeant Floyd Monument
Sioux City, IA

100-foot-high monument marks
Sgt. Floyd's final burial site.

Sergeant Floyd River Museum and Welcome Center
1000 Larsen Park Road, Sioux City, IA 51103-4914

(712) 279-0198

River transportation, Lewis and Clark.

Lewis and Clark Interpretive Center
900 Larsen Park Road, Sioux City, IA 51102

(712) 224-5242

Educational displays and hands-on activities for all ages.

Ponca State Park
88119 Spur 26-E, Ponca, NE 68770-0688

(402) 755-2284

Situated on one of the few segments of the
Missouri River that remain in a relatively natural state.
Displays on natural and cultural history.

Lewis and Clark Lake Regional Visitor Center
Highway 121, Yankton, SD 57078

(402) 667-2546

History of the Missouri River, Lewis and Clark,
U.S. Army Corps of Engineers

Lewis & Clark Information Center
Chamberlain-Oacoma, SD

(605) 734-4562 or (605) 773-3301

Displays tell of the expedition's
adventures in South Dakota.

Akta Lakota Museum
PO Box 89, Chamberlain, SD 57325

(605) 734-3452

Interpretative information on the history,
heritage, and culture of the Yankton and Teton Sioux.

The North Dakota Lewis & Clark Interpretive Center
PO Box 607, Washburn, ND 58577-0607

(701) 462-8535

Recreated 1804-1805 winter quarters,
extensive Lewis and Clark interpretation.

Knife River Indian Villages National Historic Site
PO Box 9, Stanton, ND   58571

(701) 745-3309

Visitor center, exhibits, and history and nature
trails provide interpretive information on the
Hidatsa, Mandan and Arikara.

Lewis and Clark National Historic Trail
Interpretive Center
PO Box 1806, Great Falls, MT   59403-1806

(406) 727-8733

Extensive interpretation on the entire expedition with
particular emphasis on the Great Falls portage.

Beaverhead County Museum
15 S Montana Street, Dillon, MT   59725

(406) 683-5027

Local and state history, Lewis and Clark.

Lolo Trail Center
U.S. Highway 12 West, Lolo, MT
PO Box 386, Stevensville, MT   59870

(406) 273-2201

History of the Nez Perce Trail, Lewis and Clark.

DeVoto Memorial Cedar Grove
U.S. Highway 12, ID

Picnic area named after journal editor Bernard DeVoto.

Canoe Camp
U.S. Highway 12, Orofino, ID

Canoe replica at site where canoes were made to
complete journey to the Pacific Ocean. Administered by
the Nez Perce National Historical Park.

Nez Perce National Historical Park
39063 U.S. Highway 95, Spalding, ID   83540-9715

(208) 843-2261

Visitor center and museum provide interpretive
information on the Nez Perce and regional history.

Columbia Gorge Discovery Center
5000 Discovery Drive, The Dalles, OR   97058

(541) 296-8600

Columbia River and cultural history,
some Lewis and Clark information.

The Columbia Gorge Interpretive Center
PO Box 396, Stevenson, WA   98648

(800) 991-2338

Cultural and area history,
some Lewis and Clark information.

Lewis and Clark Interpretive Center
Fort Canby State Park
PO Box 488, Ilwaco, WA   98624

(360) 642-3029

Visitor center focuses on the expedition and
provides a spectacular view of the Pacific Ocean.

Fort Clatsop National Memorial
92343 Fort Clatsop Road, Astoria, OR   97103

(503) 861-2471

Visitor center, trails, and recreated winter quarters
interpret entire journey with emphasis on the
winter of 1805-1806.

The Salt Works
Lewis and Clark Way, Seaside, OR

Recreated site where salt was made during
the winter of 1805-1806. Administered by
Fort Clatsop National Memorial.

Pompeys Pillar National Historic Landmark
PO Box 36800, Billings, MT   59107

(406) 875-2233

Site where Clark carved his name in sandstone.

Recommended Books, Web Sites, Etc.

REGARDING PLANTS AND ANIMALS

Pioneering Naturalists, by Paul Russell Cutright
   Focuses on the natural history of the expedition, including lists of plant and animal discoveries.

The Natural History of the Lewis and Clark Expedition, by Raymond Darwin Burroughs
   Information and journal quotes on the wildlife of the expedition.

Wildflowers of Washington, by C.P. Lyons
Trees and Shrubs of Washington, by C.P. Lyons
   Identification guides with an emphasis on early explorer/botanists to the region, including Lewis and Clark.

The Academy of Natural Sciences Lewis and Clark Herbarium
www.inform.umd.edu/EdRes/Colleges/LFSC/life_sciences/.plant_biology/L&C/L&Cpublic.html
   Beautiful color photos of Lewis and Clark plants.

USGS Northern Prairie Wildlife Research Center
www.npwrc.usgs.gov/resource/2000/bmam/birds.htm
www.npwrc.usgs.gov/resource/2000/bmam/mammals.htm
   Information, including illustrations and photos, on Lewis and Clark birds and mammals in North Dakota.

REGARDING NATIVE AMERICANS

Lewis and Clark among the Indians, by James Ronda
   Examines the expedition's interactions with Native Americans.

People of the First Man: Life Among the Plains in their Final Days of Glory—The First Account of Prince Maximilian's Expedition up the Missouri River, 1833-34, edited by Davis Thomas and Karin Ronnefeldt
   Watercolors by artist Karl Bodmer, text by Prince Maximilian zu Wied.

Knife River Indian Villages National Historic Site
www.nps.gov/knri/
   A great site for learning more about the Upper Missouri River Tribes. Includes teacher's guide.

Peabody Museum of Archeology and Ethnology, Harvard University
www.peabody.harvard.edu/Lewis_and_Clark/objects.html
   Contains photos of expedition artifacts and similar items.

REGARDING PERIOD MUSIC

Fiddle Tunes from the American Revolution, by Kate Van Winkle Keller
   From the personal notebook of Captain George Bush, an officer in the Continental Army.

A Choice Selection of American Country Dances of the Revolutionary Era 1775-1795,
by Kate Van Winkle Keller and Ralph Sweet
   Music and directions for 29 country dances. Accompaniment tapes also available.

www.cruzatte.com
   Site on all things musical in relation to the expedition, compiled by fiddler Daniel Slosberg, writer and performer of "Pierre Cruzatte: A Musical Journey Along the Lewis & Clark Trail."

Regarding Period Equipment, Clothing, Firearms, and Methods

Firearms, Traps, & Tools of the Mountain Men, by Carl P. Russell
Comprehensive guide to equipment used from the early 1800s to the middle 1840s.

Muzzleloader Magazine's Books of Buckskinning, I-VII
Volumes devoted to the skills and crafts of early mountain men.

Lewis & Clark: Tailor Made, Trail Worn, by Robert J. Moore, Jr. and Michael Haynes
Illustrated book on the clothing, weapons, and accessories of the expedition.

For Children

How We Crossed the West: The Adventures of Lewis and Clark, by Rosalyn Schanzer
Folk art illustrations and journal quotes tell the story of the expedition. Lower elementary grades.

The Incredible Journey of Lewis and Clark, by Rhoda Blumberg
Well-written volume for middle elementary grades.

The Lewis and Clark Coloring Book, by Peter Copeland
Forty-five captioned illustrations cover the high points of the expedition. Middle elementary through adult.

Kids Discover: Lewis and Clark, Stella Sands, editor
Activities and colorful illustrations in a magazine format (19 pages) for elementary grades.

The Book of Indian Crafts and Indian Lore, by Julian Harris Salomon
Collection of Native American crafts and activities first published in 1928. Appropriate for all grades.

General Information

Undaunted Courage: Meriwether Lewis, Thomas Jefferson, and the Opening of the American West,
by Stephen E. Ambrose
The story of the expedition in an informative, fast-paced style.

Fort Clatsop National Memorial
www.nps.gov/focl
Provides a wealth of information on the expedition.

Lewis & Clark on the Information Superhighway
www.lcarchive.org
A list of web sites related to the Lewis and Clark Expedition, compiled by Jay Rasmussen.

Jefferson National Expansion Memorial
www.nps.gov/jeff/LewisClark2/HomePage/HomePage.htm
Extensive educational site.

Lewis and Clark: The Journey of the Corps of Discovery, PBS documentary by Dayton Duncan and Ken Burns
Extraordinary four-hour video on two tapes.

PBS Online—Inside the Corps
www.pbs.org/lewisandclark/inside/index.html
Expedition information, including articles on all members of the permanent party.

Supplemental Resources

The following suppliers carry food products, period articles, and other items referred to in this book.

Bob's Red Mill Natural Foods
5209 SE International Way, Milwaukie, OR   97222

(800) 349-2173
www.bobsredmill.com

Carries corn grits, beans, barley flour, bean flour.

Azure Standard
79709 Dufur Valley Road, Dufur, OR   97021

(541) 467-2230
www.azurestandard.com

Carries corn grits, beans, barley flour, bean flour.

Following are three trail-state suppliers of buffalo meat:

Kansas Bison Company
PO Box 128, Halstead, KS   67056

(888) 835-8188
www.kansasbison.com

The Bison Ranch
7350 21st Street SE, Pingree, ND   58476

(701) 252-9711
www.thebisonranch.com

Buffalo Meat Direct
HC 40 Miles City, MT   59301

(866) 879-2833
www.buffalo-meat-direct.com

Wapato Pawn & Trade
201 S Wapato Avenue, Wapato, WA   98951

(509) 877-6405

*Deer toes, leather goods,
beading, and leather-working supplies.*

Fort Clatsop Historical Association
92343 Fort Clatsop Road, Astoria, OR   97103

(503) 861-4452
www.nps.gov/focl/catalog.htm

*Quill pens and powdered ink, jew's harps,
candle molds, flint and steel, trade items.*

Jas. Townsend & Son, Inc.
PO Box 415, Pierceton, IN   46562

(800) 338-1665
www.jastown.com

*Reproduction trade items and period supplies, including
tableware, traveling inkstands, and storage tins.*

The Lewis and Clark Trail Heritage Foundation, incorporated in 1969, supports "education, research, development, and preservation of the Lewis and Clark experience." To learn how you can become a member and receive their quarterly magazine, contact:

Lewis and Clark Trail Heritage Foundation, Inc.
PO Box 3434, Great Falls, MT   59403

(406) 454-1234
www.lewisandclark.org

Index

Page numbers in italics indicate illustrations.

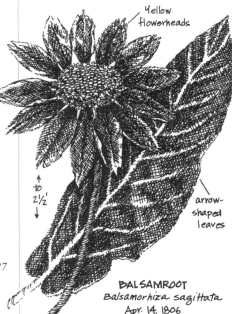

Yellow flowerheads

arrow-shaped leaves

to 2½'

BALSAMROOT
Balsamorhiza sagittata
Apr. 14, 1806

Wasco
CARVED BOWL
Made from the horn of a bighorn sheep. Circa 1800; approximately 8" in diameter.

(Columbia Gorge Discovery Center, The Dalles, OR)

NOOTKA ROSE
Rosa nutkana
June 10, 1806

pink blooms

to 10'

hips

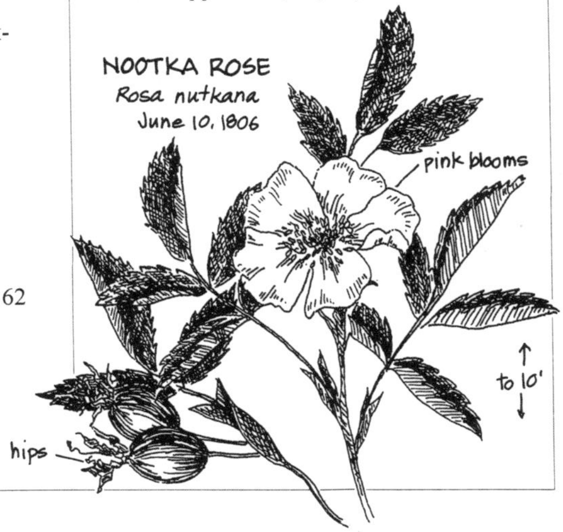

spent blooms
form fuzzy
"tassels."

TASSELS
Geum triflorum
June 12, 1806

Also called
OLD MAN'S WHISKERS

Missouri Indians, 22, 49
Missouri River, 15, 19, 33, 44, 49, 51, 64, 83-86, 106-109, 111
moccasins, *62, 97, 100, 101*
monkey flower, Lewis's, *66*
mortar and pestle, *74*
mosquitoes, 77, 83
Multnomah Indians, 23
music, 49, 56, 57, 65-68, 87, 107, 108
musket, *18*

N

Native Americans, 8, 12, 22-24, 26, 27, 45, 49-52, 54-57, 59-70, 74-76, 80, 81, 85, 86, 88-93, 95-97, 100-103, 106-108, 110, 122; as guides, 60, 88; supplying food for Corps, 44, 52, 75, 76, 92, 93, 102, 103
Newfoundland (dog), 39, *40*
Nez Perce, 22, 46, 63, 68, 70, 74-76, 80, 88, 93, 95, 106; beadwork, *24;* hat, *22;* mortar and pestle, *74;* parfleche, *110*
Nucifraga columbiana, 36
Numenius americanus, 85
nutcracker, Clark's, *36,* 77
nuts, 44, 93

O

oak, Oregon white, *92*
oars, *83*
octant, *34*
Odocoileus hemionus, 79
old man's whiskers, *124*
Omaha Indians, 22
Oncorhynchus mykiss, 91
onions, wild, 44
Opuntia polyacantha, 86
Ordway, John, 14, 17, 20, 52, 56, 57, 84, 111
Oreamnos americanus, 88
Oregon grape, *125*
Oregon sunshine, *39*
Osage Indians, 22
Osage orange, *20*
Oto Indians, 22, 49
Ovis canadensis, 84
owl, Montana horned, *82*

P

Pacific Ocean, 15, 25, 33, 90, 93, 94, 102
paddles, canoe, *95, 98*
Palouse Indians, 23
parfleche, *110*
Pawnee Indians, 22
pawpaw, 44, 107, *109*
Pelecanus erythrorhynchos, 85
pelican, white, *85*
pemmican, 44
penknife, *37*
permanent party, 15-17, 64
pestle, stone, *74*
phacelia, linear-leaved, *31*
Phacelia linearis, 31
Philadelphus lewisii, 36
phlox, showy, *10*
Phlox speciosa, 10
Pica pica hudsonia, 64
Picea engelmannii, 71
Picea sitchensis, 99
pigtail tobacco, 23
pine: lodgepole, *70,* 92; ponderosa, *71, 76, 89,* 93; western white, *71, 96;* whitebark, *70*
Pinus albicaulis, 70
Pinus contorta, 70

Pinus monticola, 71, 96
Pinus ponderosa, 71, 89
pirogues, *43,* 64
Pituophis sayi sayi, 79
plant press, *30*
plants, 26-31; number of new to science, 15, 20; *see also* flowers, shrubs, trees
platform, dip-net, *91*
plum, wild, 44
Pompeys Pillar, *106*
Populus deltoides, 51
Populus trichocarpa, 31
portable soup, 72, 73
portage, 64, 83, 86, 87, 89, 90
pottery, Mandan/Hidatsa, *58,* 64
Potts, John, 17
powder horn, *32*
prairie dog, black-tailed, 64, *77,* 108
prickly pear, plains, *86*
pronghorn, 77, *79*
provisions, 39, 41, 72, 73, 107, 109
Prunus virginiana, 60
Pryor, Nathaniel, 17, 20
Pseudotsuga menziesii, 70, 98
Purshia tridentata, 113

Q

Quercus garryana, 92
quill pen, *37*
quillwork (porcupine), 24, *63*

R

rattle, *57;* Plains deer-toe, *56;* Plains rawhide, *57*
rattlesnake, 46, 77, 108; northern Pacific (skin & rattle), *46*
recreation, 68
redcedar, western, *70, 95, 98*
reference books (carried on the expedition), 28, 34
Ribes aureum, 44
Ribes cereum, 26
rings (as gifts), 23
Rocky Mountains, 50, 59, 69-72, 74, 75, 83, 88, 89, 108
root bag, Yakama, 26
roots, *44, 61, 75, 76, 93, 97, 102*
Rosa nutkana, 123
rose, Nootka, *123*

yellow
blooms

glossy
leaves

dark blue berries
with powdery white "bloom"

OREGON GRAPE
mahonia aquifolium
Apr. 11, 1806

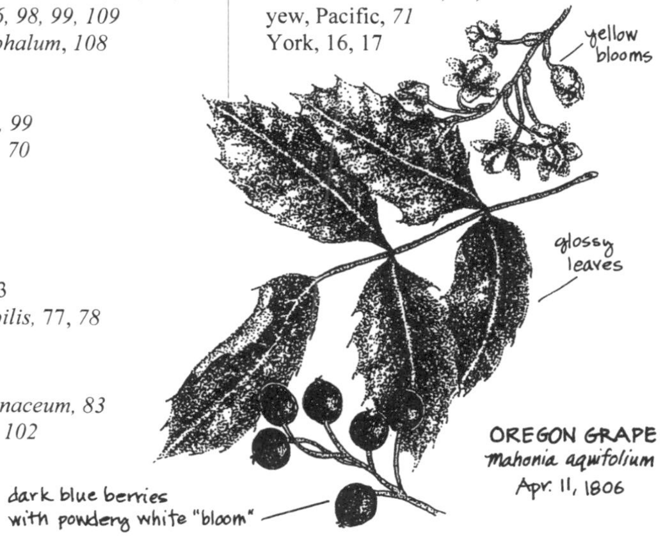

To obtain additional copies of
this book or the musical CD
Lewis and Clark: Songs of the Journey,
contact:

Edge of the Woods
PO Box 8251
Yakima, WA   98908

edgeofthewoods@nwinfo.net

Also available:
***Lewis and Clark:
Songs of the Journey Accompaniment***
An accompaniment-only CD suitable
for sing-alongs and classroom
performances.